A Preview and

Summary of

"The Wayward Welfare State"

★ ★ ★ ★ ★ ★ ★ ★ ★ ★ ★ ★ *A Preview and Summary of "The Wayward Welfare State"*

Roger A. Freeman

Hoover Institution Press
Stanford University, Stanford, California

Hoover Press Publication 257

©1981 by the Board of Trustees of the
   Leland Stanford Junior University
All rights reserved
International Standard Book Number: 0-8179-7572-1
Library of Congress Catalog Card Number: 81-81358
Printed in the United States of America

★ ★ ★ ★ ★ ★ ★ ★ ★ ★ ★ ★ ★ ★ ★ ★ ★ ★ *Contents*

★ ★ ★ ★ ★ ★ ★ ★ ★ ★ ★ ★ ★ ★ ★ ★ ★ ★ *Preface*

Government is not the solution to our problem; government is the problem. . . .

It is my intention to curb the size and influence of the federal establishment. . . .

President Ronald W. Reagan
Inaugural address, January 20, 1981

The term *welfare state* has in recent years acquired a negative, almost pejorative, connotation. For generations the dream of the future of the political left, the welfare state was first carried into reality by the political right. Otto von Bismarck established compulsory social insurance in the 1880s—to take the wind out of the sails of the socialists—and Winston Churchill during World War II commissioned Sir William Beveridge to design the first "cradle to grave" security plan, probably for reasons similar to Bismarck's. It seems an irony that both, Bismarck and Churchill, were driven from office not too long after they became patrons of the welfare state. For most of the past century, it was the political left which fought and bled for, established and expanded the major programs which constitute the building blocks of the welfare state. Its ideas were adopted and instituted in most industrial nations within half a century; over the succeeding fifty years they were also embraced by most of the less developed countries, in principle, if not always in economic reality.

It was its triumph of being nearly universally welcomed, adopted, and enormously expanded that made the welfare state a victim of its own success, brought about its troubles, its loss of luster and, through attitudinal and political changes in some Western countries, its fall from grace.

The exuberance of the 1960s in the United States visualized a multiplication and intensification of social programs as a certain and effective cure for nearly all social ills. It set out to attain the millennium well before the millennial year 2000. But it soon tripped along the rocky road. Initial enthusiasm promoted programs founded on noble but vastly exaggerated hopes and on ignorance or disregard of the reality of human nature. Unrealistic expectations were bound to be disappointed and by their failure generated unfavorable to hostile reactions. The welfare state was led astray by splendid intentions and daydreams which turned it into the *wayward welfare state*,[1] as I called it some years ago and now choose as the title of this volume.

The idea for this book originated in the mid-1960s. I had then been studying governmental problems such as taxes, education, welfare, the military, intergovernmental relations, and dealing with them, in the White House and at a governor's office for about fifteen years. My responsibilities required me to focus on the broad aspects, on budget and economic policies, on priorities in resource allocation, on the potentials and consequences of major programs. After extensively writing in several of those fields, I decided to prepare a comprehensive treatment of public affairs.

I presented a paper "The Service State at the Midcentury" to the annual conference of the American Society for Public Administration (ASPA) in 1965 and subsequently rewrote it for the *National Review* (September 21, 1965). Early in 1966, I restructured and expanded the ASPA paper, at Seymour Harris' invitation, into a speech "Big Government—Friend or Foe," which I delivered at the San Diego Open Forum. For that widely reprinted speech, the Freedoms Foundation at Valley Forge accorded me its George Washington Honor Medal Award as "an outstanding accomplishment in helping to achieve a better understanding of the American Way of Life." I prepared a new version of the theme in 1970 as keynote address for the annual conference of the Governmental Research Association. It was reprinted several times and earned a George Washington Honor Medal Award from the Freedoms Foundation for a summary in *The New York Times* of December 4, 1971.

I then received several suggestions to turn the paper into a comprehensive research project on "The Growth of American Government." Under that heading it was approved by the Hoover Institution on War, Revolution and Peace and occupied much of my time for several years. Urgent requests for special studies, reports, analyses, articles and speeches of current topical interest and periods of public service interfered and delayed completion.

The Growth of American Government was published by the Hoover Institution in 1975, was widely reviewed and received the Governmental Research Association's *Most Distinguished Research Award* for 1975.

The size of government and its rate of growth had not been much in the forefront of public interest prior to 1975 but was then beginning to attract increasing attention. After *Newsweek* filled the cover of its December 15, 1975, issue with the picture of a grotesquely bloated Uncle Sam, under the caption BIG GOVERNMENT, other media followed with extensive coverage and *Big Government* became a focal subject of the 1976 presidential campaign. It has remained in the center of interest ever since, with attitudes toward it, positive or negative, often serving as the dividing line between the ideological and political right and left.

Governmental expansion did not, as it sometimes seems, originate in the 1960s or 1950s, nor in the Great Depression of the 1930s. Scope and magnitude of governmental programs have been growing for a much longer time, as Solomon Fabricant so effectively demonstrated in *The Trend of Government Activity in the United States Since 1900*, a comprehensive analysis of the vast expansion in the size and function of government during the first half of the twentieth century.[2] His study was based on data from 1900 to 1949. M. Slade Kendrick, in *A Century and a Half of Federal Expenditures* carried federal expenditure data historically back to 1789 and forward to 1952.[3] Fabricant as well as Kendrick found and reported a consistent upward trend in public spending and concluded that it would continue as far as one could see ahead.

The Growth of American Government is a critical analysis of governmental activities in the years 1952 to 1972, a period that covered developments from the later stages of the Korean War to the later stages of the Vietnam War.

After reprinting the volume several times, the Hoover Institution asked me in 1979 to bring the book up-to-date. I soon realized that a mere updating would not do. Too much happened in the intervening six years, in terms of programs, political changes, research studies and public attitudes. Moreover, I felt that several subjects now required a more thorough explanation and discussion than I had prepared in 1974. Above all, several issues that then seemed less important and were barely mentioned, have since acquired great significance. New chapters and sections had to be written. In other words, this is an entirely new book, in title as well as substance. Its basic thesis has not changed but as the new title indicates, its emphasis has shifted further from a consideration of the magnitude of government to a critical review of the nature and consequences of its activities. Research and the writing of this book took well over a year, which may explain why some parts are updated to a more recent date than others.

The charitable approach of the welfare state—the idea that government should help the less fortunate among its citizens cope with some of the major hazards of life, which demonstrably they cannot meet by alernative means without such aid—has been generally accepted. It is no longer controversial. Nor would anyone in a position of responsibility, now or in the foreseeable future, want to dismantle our social security system and its major components—or could if he tried. The system needs reform, not repeal. What is at issue is not the welfare state as such but the *wayward* welfare state.

In program after program, assistance to individuals who for manifest and tangible reasons were faced with insuperable problems, turned out to be the proverbial camel's nose in the tent. Definitions of need were broadened so as to include vastly larger numbers, to add political support to that of an initially narrow group of eligible recipients. Benefits were adjusted to attract a less than poorest-of-the-poor clientele. To labor at arduous or menial jobs became less necessary or urgent for unskilled persons of low-productive and therefore low-earning capacity. With the work ethic but a faint memory of bygone days, social problems multiplied exponentially—from family breakup to evasion of support responsibility and to all types of violent and property crime.

Increasingly, the welfare state shaped its tax and spending policies to pursue egalitarian ideas and made redistribution of income—from those who earn it to those who yearn it—its foremost goal. To punish effort and success and reward indolence and failure, even if not so intended, takes an inevitable toll on the growth potential of a dynamic economy. Other indirect effects of the wayward welfare state may have no less serious—and possibly more ominous—consequences. Ever more generous social benefits pushed government outlays up faster than the prevailing rate of economic growth. Between 1952 and 1978 aggregate governmental expenditures multiplied sevenfold, Gross National Product (GNP) sixfold. Inflation, caused by excessive public spending and resulting huge budgetary deficits meanwhile cut the purchasing power of the 1978 dollar to 40 cents of the 1952 dollar (by 1981 to 29 cents). Expressed in *constant* (price-adjusted) dollars, government expenditures multiplied 3.0-fold between 1952 and 1978, GNP 2.3-fold.

But this tells only part of the story. The federal government—disregarding for the moment state and local government outlays—expended in the early 1950s four times as much for national defense as for domestic services and benefits. In the late 1970s it was spending nearly three times as much for domestic functions as for defense. The share of national defense dropped from 49% of all governmental outlays (federal, state, local) in 1952 to 16% in 1978. The share of domestic outlays meanwhile doubled, from 38% to 76%.

Reduction to one-third of their former share in national resources has had a devastating impact on the ability of our Armed Forces to deal with emergencies, on their readiness to cope with broader challenges that may arise on short notice or none. America's military strength fell from unquestioned superiority a quarter century ago to a condition where in many or most respects it is inferior to the power the Soviet Union can array against us.

What did we get in return for a perilous weakening of our national security? A sixfold increase (*constant* dollars) in governmental spending for domestic functions between 1952 and 1978. That means that a population, 39% larger than it was a quarter century earlier, consumed 498% more in outlays for welfare, income maintenance, education, medical care and a myriad of other domestic services.

The past few decades have seen a drastic change in the nature of American government. Public opinion polls and elections suggest that a majority of the American people no longer favor the trends outlined above—if it ever did. There seems to be a broad national consensus that our defense capability needs to be significantly strengthened and the expansion of other major public programs restrained. The adjustment process will not be easy and may be painful. Expectations may change from the "soaring sixties" a couple of decades ago to the "sobering eighties." Whether the changes outlined above will actually take place within the critical next decade or two no one can foretell. I hope that this book may contribute to a better understanding of what has been happening in and to the United States over the past quarter century—and what could or may happen if we refuse to learn from the lessons of the past.

The Wayward Welfare State turned into a bigger book than I had originally envisaged and its publication is taking longer than I anticipated. It therefore seemed advisable to publish in advance of the book itself, this *Preview and Summary* which presents its main ideas and factual findings in a more concise form.

I am deeply grateful to W. Glenn Campbell, director of the Hoover Institution, for his interest in and unstinted support of the project, to Dennis L. Bark, deputy director, for guiding the manuscript through the publications department, to Richard T. Burress, associate director and chairman of the publications committee, and to those of my Hoover colleagues who reviewed chapters or sections of the manuscript and were helpful in offering suggestions, giving me advice and commenting on my ideas and their presentation. This includes especially Martin Anderson, Michael Block, Rita Ricardo-Campbell, Paul Hanna, Sidney Hook, Richard Muth, Fred Nold, Alvin Rabushka, Dan Throop Smith and Thomas Sowell. Benyam Mulugeta assisted me by extensive library research, statistical work and in many other ways, through much of the time this book was in preparation. Anna Boberg did most of the typing and proofing with her usual speed, precision, as well as library work, except for two months of world travel during which time Linda Sandham filled her place. Maria Jedd prepared the graphs with understanding and technical skill.

I owe thanks to all of them. Responsibility for the facts I present and for the opinion I express remains, of course, exclusively my own.

Stanford, California   Roger A. Freeman

★★★★★ A Preview and Summary

If a nation values anything more than freedom, it will lose its freedom; and the irony of it is that if it is comfort or money that it values more, it will lose that too.

Somerset Maugham[4]

The birth of the American welfare state in the 1930s, and its dramatic expansion during the third quarter of the twentieth century may, in historical perspective, have been among the most significant developments of our time. To its architects, the maturing of the welfare state has been a matter of supreme pride and immense satisfaction. It means to them that compassion is replacing the law of the economic jungle, that the American people have finally, later than leading European nations, come to recognize and discharge their obligation toward the less fortunate in their midst, that they are willing and ready to make distributive social justice a reality.

Some aspects of the welfare state are now regarded as integral components of a twentieth century industrial society and have been adopted by most western countries. Social insurance against major hazards of life such as old age, death of the breadwinner, unemployment, medical emergencies is no longer controversial *in principle*, though their financing and benefit structures inevitably are. Assumption by the state of much of the responsibility formerly borne by voluntary charity or community action, for relief to individuals and families which through no fault of their own are in distress, is now taken for granted.

It was not the basic idea of the welfare state, of helping victims of misfortune, but its excesses, which David Stockman in 1975 called the "social pork barrel"[5] that caused the American public gradually to cool off and give the term welfare state a derogatory flavor. Activation of hundreds of programs and policies which were promoted as cures for all types of social ills but failed to produce the promised improvements, spread disillusionment. It engendered growing resentment when the results of such attempts at social engineering and egalitarian redistribution and the enormous cost of those schemes could no longer be hidden. Some of the manifestations of the welfare state were increasingly viewed as an abandonment of the foundations upon which this nation was built—as a renunciation of the principle of personal responsibility and a system of rewards and punishment that made this country grow from wilderness to the world's most advanced and prosperous within two centuries. The avenue leading to the welfare state began increasingly to look like the *Road to Serfdom* which Friedrich A. Hayek had described three decades earlier. The welfare state of the 1970s became to its critics a symbol as well as a cause and mark of the decline and eventual fall of a great nation whose latter-day offspring rejected its promise, forsook its destiny and squandered their birthright.

The American welfare state is a creature of the New Deal: its ideological, political and constitutional-legal foundations, its infrastructure and technology were thought out and shaped in the days of Franklin Roosevelt and the Great Depression. But the reality of the welfare state as we know it now, was not and could not have been established in the 1930s because there simply wasn't enough money available from government revenues, nor were budget deficits of the magnitude we have since come to know, deemed tolerable.

Even in the early 1950s, twenty years after the coming of the New Deal, federal spending for all domestic functions totaled only $12 billion a year. A quarter century later it approached $300 billion. How was it possible to *increase financing each year* by an average of over $10 billion—almost as much as it had taken 163 years—from 1789 to 1952—to reach? It took World War II and inflation to make this possible. Early in the war, income taxes were boosted to previously unthinkable levels and accepted by the public as part of a national emergency, an inevitable but temporary burden. After the war ended, taxes were only slightly lowered and the resulting and rapidly multiplying receipts were channeled into income transfer and social service programs. It is inconceivable that Congress could have enacted or that the American people would have countenanced tax boosts of the size needed to fund the social programs of the 1960s and 1970s. Wartime tax rates adusted the taxpaying public psychologically and economically to confiscatory tax rates. Thus it regarded the minor reductions after 1945 as welcome relief and settled for them, though grumbling at their inadequacy.

As so often, the taste of "free" government money only whetted the appetite of claimants: widespread demands and congressional response by enlarged appropriations grew exponentially. During the 1950s and 1960s and into the 1970s the welfare state was financed largely by cutting national defense from a two-thirds share of the federal budget to less than one-fourth and from 13.5% of Gross National Product (GNP) to 5%. The Soviet Union which in the 1950s devoted a slightly smaller percentage of GNP to its armed forces than the U.S. has since pursued an ambitious armament program which boosted the share of the military to 13% of GNP in the late 1970s and, according to some American experts, to 18% in 1980. Although the Russians produce only about half as big a GNP as we, they spend the equivalent of about 50% more than we on their armed forces. Small wonder that the military supremacy of the United States, unquestioned for many years, dwindled to a point where the United States is now, in several major categories, militarily inferior to the Soviet Union. Russian leaders do not make such huge and growing investments, year after year, without a clear purpose in mind. Their activities and show of force in several continents make it evident that their eventual goal is nothing short of Soviet world domination.

When sometime in the 1970s it became more widely realized that the share of resources allocated to U.S. national security had been allowed to fall below minimum safety, the shift from the defense to the domestic budget ended; the well had run dry. But the momentum of the giant social programs was built into the system and the growth of most of those outlays became, to use technical budget term, "uncontrollable." With outgo continuing to head upward but a major source of funds, defense, cut off, a succession of huge budgetary deficits became a regular and inevitable fact of federal finances. Back-to-back monetarized deficits were not the only but the most potent force that drove inflation rates to two-digit levels which proved impervious to presidential and congressional oratory.

At the end of the 1970s annual inflation rates reached 13%. At that

3

rate, if continued, the dollar would be worth about a nickel of its 1980 value by the end of the century. But what makes us so confident that the rate could not go up to 15%, 20% or more? History gives ample examples of inflation rates in the hundreds and thousands—and of eventual ruin, not only of an economy but a nation.

Lasting and worsening inflation contributed to a growing antagonism toward the welfare state as its root cause. The multiplication of governmental activities, their intrusion into everyday affairs and the tightening control exercised by a central bureaucracy fueled an anti-big-government sentiment which became evident in the 1976 presidential campaign. Never before had the size of government been so much in the forefront of nationwide interest.

In the Republican primaries of 1976 both candidates declared their preference for less rather than more government and they wound up in a photo finish. On the Democratic side, thirteen out of fourteen candidates advocated "improvement," i.e., expansion of existing programs and the enactment of new ones. Only one of the fourteen candidates, Jimmy Carter, announced that he was running against big government in Washington and promised to shrink it, if given an opportunity. He ran without the support and even against opposition from within his party's organization. But he won, first in the primaries, then in the election.

As it turned out, the growth rate of federal domestic spending dropped substantially during the four years of the Carter administration. Was this the result of a policy to carry out campaign promises? It hardly seems so. Within four weeks of assuming office, President Carter sent to Congress revisions in President Ford's 1978 budget which upped budget authority by $29.5 billion while cutting defense by $2.7 billion. Most of the increases were for social programs and the President commented in his message that "they are important first steps toward a federal government that is more effective and more responsive to our people's needs." He subsequently proposed major new programs in public welfare, medical care, education, housing, etc. which would have added multibillion amounts if they had been enacted by Congress, which most of them were not.

The most plausible explanation for the slower growth of domestic spending in the late 1970s may well be that the money simply was not there. Defense was no longer available as a major source of funds. Budgetary deficits, an alternative source, reached new heights at levels which for political and economic reasons could not be exceeded. Tax

4

boosts, except for social security and on oil "windfall" profits seemed unacceptable. This suggests that force of necessity more than a frugal presidential or congressional policy slowed the growth rate of federal domestic spending during the Carter regime.

By all appearances though, federal activities, especially regulatory, kept expanding through the 1970s, and so did public attitude against big government. The strength of that sentiment seems to have been confirmed in the 1980 presidential and congressional elections. They were widely hailed as a landmark and turning point in a trend toward bigger government that had been evident for several decades. How certain can we be about the meaning or "mandate" of the 1980 elections?

The vote certainly indicated a widespread desire to "get government off our backs," expressed unhappiness with double-digit inflation, heavy taxes, overregulation, a high-handed bureaucracy, a weakening of our military capability, resulting loss of standing in the world and the national leadership's obvious impotence in dealing with international emergencies.

Does the vote in November 1980 also mean that the American people want a strengthening of national defense sufficiently to accept offsetting reductions in domestic expenditures? Are they ready to approve cutbacks in the range and extent of governmental services? That is far from certain. Public opinion polls in recent years have shown that respondents want government to spend less. In a June 1978 Gallup poll 84% of respondents voted that the federal government is spending too much and 76% that the government in Washington is too powerful. But substantial majorities simultaneously favored spending more to fight crime, improve health care, education, etc. A February 1980 Gallup poll showed a similar picture. Nearly four out of five would support a constitutional amendment to force balancing the federal budget but equal or larger majorities want to maintain or increase government spending for a large number of public services. Only foreign aid and welfare—which means public assistance but does not include social security benefits for the aged—are popular targets for cutbacks.

The trouble with those polls is that they offer respondents an opportunity to vote for more money for police and fire departments, schools, medical care, sanitation, parks and other services but no chance to say that what they really want is not, for example, more money for education but more education for the money, not higher salaries for policemen but more effective protection against crime, etc. Experience in recent decades has shown that allocating more money to a program does not always produce desired results. Better schools or crime control may call for various types of action but not necessarily for more money. Nor is additional money an adequate substitute for the sometimes tough and widely unpopular steps required to bring better results.

Most polls leave the crucial questions unanswered and disclose an ambivalent attitude: people seem to want government to spend less in the aggregate, but more for each of their favorite services. That does not give public officials clear policy directions. When movements arise to restrain government growth and increased spending, the numerous special interest groups, each with a stake in a particular field, combine forces—"gang up"—and more often than not are able to prevent legislative action that could jeopardize their goals and economic fortunes.

There is clear evidence that the people were willing, at least for several decades, to tax themselves more heavily for improved services. At state and local levels voters exert far more influence on taxes than at the federal level, because most tax boosts and bond issues require prior approval at the ballot box. Yet, state and local taxes jumped from 8.4% of GNP in 1952 to 15.1% in 1978. This might at first glance suggest that local public services and their financing could best be left to the decisions of states and communities. But this runs up against the enormous popularity of federal money which seems to come for free. Governors, legislators or mayors do not have to accept political responsibility for boosting federal taxes. Moreover, the federal tax burden has remained amazingly stable for decades. Federal revenues equaled 21.2% of GNP in 1952, 21.4% in 1978. Automatic increases in receipts due to economic growth and inflation were offset by periodic reductions in the federal income tax rates, which succeeded in keeping the tax load on an even level.

In the second half of the 1970s, as public sentiment turned against governmental growth, the period of steep tax boosts at state and local levels came to a screeching halt. A taxpayers' revolt broke out, symbolized by California's proposition 13 in June 1978 which cut property taxes in half. The tax revolt had only limited success in other states. With few exceptions it did not go very far and the failure of the majority of tax cut proposals on November 1980 state ballots suggests that the tax revolt may have fizzled out. However, the prospect for

6

resuming big tax boosts at state and local levels appears slim and this directs attention for greater funds again at the federal government.

That the federal tax burden remained stable over the past quarter century, at about 21 percent of GNP as mentioned above, may come as a surprise to many otherwise well-informed persons. Everybody knows that federal spending has been soaring in recent decades, far outpacing the growth rate of the nation's economy. Everybody also knows that the federal bureaucracy has dramatically expanded, at a much faster rate than the U.S. population or the civilian labor force. *Everybody, that is, who has not looked at the record.*

The fact is that federal spending has been growing only slightly faster than the nation's economy: from 20.5% of GNP in 1952 to 21.6% in 1978.

This picture of a seemingly moderate rate of growth in federal spending, however, is deceptive. It hides the fact, referred to earlier, that federal spending for domestic purposes jumped from 18% of total outlays in 1952 to 62% in 1978, while outlays for national defense fell from 65% of the budget to 24%. Now that the era during which much of the welfare state expansion could be financed by shrinking the budgetary share of defense has come to an end, the welfare state is in trouble. It cannot possibly expand at the rate at which it has grown in recent decades. In fact, if our defense establishment is to be enabled to attain again a position of military might second to none, the federal slice allocated to domestic services—at 62% of the federal budget and at 13.5% of GNP in 1978—will have to be reduced in the course of the 1980s.

The fiscal picture is somewhat complicated by the fact that several levels of government are involved as well as different types of expenditures. It might be somewhat clarified by an analysis of governmental employment.

Is the Federal Bureaucracy Mushrooming?

Whenever discussion turns to the growth of government, the magnitude of the federal bureaucracy and its rapid proliferation are prominently mentioned. The fact is that federal civilian employment, at 2.9 million in 1978, is slightly below its level ten years earlier. Between 1952 and 1978 it increased by 12% while the U.S. population meanwhile expanded 39% and private business employment 47%. But before we jump to the conclusion that federal offices are badly understaffed we might consider a few related facts.

The 12% growth in federal civilian employment covers a staff *reduction* of 26% in the Department of Defense, a combined increase of 26% in the Postal Service and the Veterans Administration—less than the rate of population growth—and an expansion of 89% in the remaining agencies, which administer the other federal domestic programs. That equals about twice the growth rate of private business employment.

But the federal payroll is only the visible part of the iceberg, the part *above* the surface, the part which presidents and other federal officials point at with pride, time and again—for public consumption. It does not include the large numbers of consultants, of work "farmed out," which does not appear in employment statistics. Moreover, most domestic public services are partially or wholly financed by the federal treasury, performed by employees of state and local governments. It is the national government that offers, finances, encourages and, to an increasing extent, mandates the programs. But those who implement them do not appear in the statistics of federal employment. Five hundred categorical grant and loan authorizations are now in operation—up from 61 in 1952—and their cost jumped from $2.6 billion in 1952 to $78 billion in 1978. Thus, if we want to get a fair picture of public employment we must take a good look at state and local government staffs.

State and local government employment increased 183% between 1952 and 1978—more than four times faster than the population and four times faster than private employment. All governmental employment in the United States (federal, state, local) increased 66%. Excluding national defense (which was cut 37%) the rate of increase was 154%. There was one nondefense employee in government for every 9.3 in private employment in 1952. There was one for every 5.4 in 1978. If that rate of growth were to continue, most of us would be on the governmental payroll early in the XXI Century. Who would then produce the goods and services we need and consume?

To put it in other terms: there were in 1952 31.3 public employees in national defense for every 1,000 persons in the population; in 1978 there were only 14.2. There were in 1952 36.6 public *non*defense employees for every 1,000 persons in the population, but 67.0 per 1,000 in 1978. So if we add defense and nondefense, the 1952 to 1978 growth is less than spectacular: from 67.9 to 81.2. The cut in defense served to hide the domestic expansion.

Figure 1
GOVERNMENTAL EMPLOYMENT BY LEVEL OF GOVERNMENT
1952 to 1978
(per 1000 population)

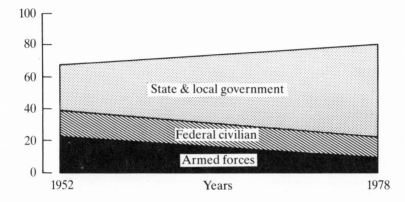

From the Warfare State to the Welfare State

What happened in public employment also happened in public expenditures. Moderate overall growth concealed a drastic shift in resources from defense to social programs. Total governmental spending in the United States (federal, state, local) multiplied sevenfold between 1952 and 1978, slightly ahead of a sixfold increase in the nation's income and product. Much of this growth was due to inflation and the increases look more modest when expressed in *constant* (price-adjusted) dollars. GNP in *real* terms grew 135%, governmental spending 197%. That 197% growth consists of a *4% decline* in national defense and a *498% growth* in domestic services: outlays for income support went up 919%, for medical care 838%, for education 487%.

The share of domestic services in the nation's public budgets doubled, from 38% in 1952 to 76% in 1978, while the share of defense fell from 49% to 16%. Personal consumption of the American people increased 153%, government consumption (domestic purposes) 498%. Back in 1952 government services claimed about one-fourth as much as individual consumers spent for their food, clothing and household operations. By 1978 Americans—at least those who paid taxes—had to hand over to government more for its various services than they laid out for their own food, clothing and household operations.

9

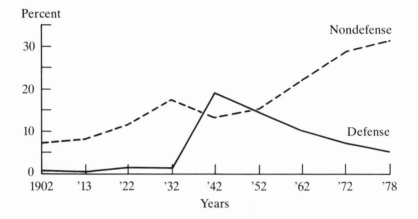

Figure 2
GOVERNMENTAL EXPENDITURES IN THE UNITED STATES
1902 to 1978
(in percent of gross national product)

This is more than a change in relative magnitudes. It is a drastic change in the nature of society and state in the United States over the past quarter century. In classical political theory, from Thomas Hobbes through John Locke to John Stuart Mill, the primary purpose and duty of the state is to protect the safety of its citizens, their lives and property, from aggressors, foreign or domestic. The secondary purpose of the state is to establish and enforce rules for the ordinary and peaceful conduct of civil affairs and to settle disputes among its citizens. Such were the tradition and goals that guided the authors of federal and state constitutions. It still expresses the beliefs of a broad majority of Americans.

Trends dating back to the nineteenth century and gaining strength during the first half of the twentieth century aimed toward a widening of the range of public functions, greater intensity in services, and perpetual growth in governmental finances and employment, as Solomon Fabricant demonstrated in *The Trend of Government Activity in the United States since 1900*. In retrospect, however, viewing the record of the 1950s, 1960s, and 1970s, these developments to mid-century were gradual and modest. The most dramatic expansion, particularly in the broad field of social welfare, took place in the third quarter of the twentieth century when government extended its

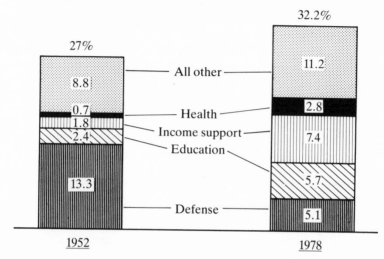

Figure 3
GOVERNMENTAL EXPENDITURES IN THE UNITED STATES, BY FUNCTION
1952 and 1978
(as a percentage of gross national product)

responsibilities for its citizens and the range of decisions over their personal lives. As government assumed and tightened control over the actions and transactions of individuals, over the conduct and management of business from small shops to giant corporations, of schools and colleges and virtually all types of private institutions, it failed increasingly to live up to responsibilities that had historically been regarded to be its foremost duties. Personal safety of citizens on the streets and in their homes became but a fond memory of bygone days, as violent and property crimes multiplied and many or most offenders went scot-free or got off cheaply. The security of the United States itself and of its lifelines to essential resources, allies, friends and other vital interests overseas which were beyond a conceivable challenge three decades ago are now increasingly threatened as America's military capacity to defend them fell to new lows.

It certainly was not so intended nor expected when the modest beginnings of a welfare state first appeared on the scene in America, nor when they were spawned in Europe half a century earlier.

Nearly a hundred years ago Otto von Bismarck introduced the idea of state protection through social insurance. Concerned over the growing power and influence of the rising business and professional classes—the *laissez-faire* liberals—in Germany's new second empire, Bismarck attempted to lure industrial workers from the social democrats to the conservatives or to form a *de facto* alliance in the Reichstag between the *junkers* (the landed aristocracy) and the political left. This axis between the statists on the right and the statists on the left was renewed on several occasions, most clearly in the Germany of the 1920s and 1930s when Nazis and Communists joined in attacks to bring down the liberal forces in the middle, the Weimar regime.

But it was only in America, where the free market tradition was stronger than in Europe that the statists in what was probably a shrewd move, usurped the label their opponents had held for so long: they became the "new liberals," though the welfare state is the very antithesis of the original liberal idea. The new liberals favored and supported the growing centralization of authority in the national government, which they viewed as a more *progressive* force than hidebound states and local communities. Only later did it become apparent that concentration of power respects individual rights no more than states rights or local autonomy. It has been said that *freedom is indivisible*. If it is taken from states or cities, citizens will soon learn that their ability to make decisions for themselves becomes increasingly limited, subject to restraint by higher levels of government.

The American welfare state has its roots in the Great Depression. In no year prior to 1930 did federal expenditures for domestic purposes come close to $1 billion. Even in the seven years of the New Deal they remained below $7 billion a year and did not reach $12 billion until 1952, twenty years after the birth of the New Deal.[6] In 1978 they totaled $287 billion.

Although its ideological and political bases were laid in the 1930s, the reality of the American welfare state was launched in the postwar period as the "Fair Deal," gathered speed in the late 1950s, and zoomed under the labels of the "New Frontier" and the "Great Society" at a breathtaking rate through the 1960s into the 1970s. Its prophet is John Kenneth Galbraith, who propounded the theory that government and its services are being scandalously starved while the private consumer luxuriates. His solution: to tax the latter more heavily to support the former more generously.[7]

The counterargument holds that the consumer, who supposedly luxuriates, only consumes the goods he produced, or their equivalent value to which he acquired title by turning out goods or services for others. But the egalitarian welfare state proponents recognize no such claim of the producer. They want to redistribute income and consumption more equally among high producers, low producers, and nonproducers, according to their own sense of social justice. They aim to overrule, through the political process, the rewards and punishments of the free market, disregarding the question of whether a society can remain free without a free market.

The case for the welfare state was presented well by George Katona of the Institute for Social Research, University of Michigan:

> This is the most serious argument against the mass consumption society: the consumer exercises his influence in a socially undesirable manner. It is Galbraith's accomplishment to have presented the argument to the American public in a most convincing way. We do not have enough schools and spend far too little on education; we do not have enough hospitals and spend far too little on the health of our people; there are too many slums which breed delinquency and crime; scarcity prevails in the entire domain of public expenditures, such as highways, parks, and recreation facilities.[8]

Galbraith as well as Katona criticized the level of public spending for domestic purposes as lamentably inadequate. Galbraith blamed this on exorbitant private consumption; Katona on excessive military outlays.

Both saw their primary goal fulfilled: governmental outlays for domestic purposes multiplied six times—in *constant* dollars—over the past quarter century, as I showed earlier. Galbraith was not able to see a reduction in the consumers' share; it remained at about 63% of GNP, although government revenues rose from 29.6% of GNP to 36.5%, with more of the funds "recycled" to consumers. Katona's ideas were carried out; the share of defense in total government spending was cut by two-thirds between 1952 and 1978. The shift in national priorities which some political and academic groups had been demanding for years, "from the warfare state to the welfare state" has taken place. What have been the results of that shift?

The Harvest of the Welfare State

President Lyndon Johnson's panegyric of the welfare state on June 26, 1964, as he was launching his multitude of programs, bears repeating:

13

We stand at the edge of the greatest era in the life of any nation. For the first time in world history we have the abundance and the ability to free every man from hopeless want, and to free every person to find fulfillment in the works of his mind or the labor of his hands.

Even the greatest of all past civilizations existed on the exploitation of the misery of the many.

This Nation, this people, this generation, has man's first chance to create a Great Society: a society of success without squalor, beauty without barrenness, works of genius without the wretchedness of poverty. We can open the doors of learning. We can open the doors of fruitful labor and rewarding leisure, of open opportunity and close community—not just to the privileged few, but, thank God, we can open those doors to everyone.[9]

Mr. Johnson's supreme confidence in the effectiveness of the programs which he maneuvered through Congress in the mid-1960s is truly astounding. To compare his magnificent promise of an inevitable triumph with the sober reality of the 1970s is pathetic. The Brookings Institution's Henry Aaron, who served as assistant secretary of HEW for planning and evaluation in the Carter administration, speculated on what a Rip Van Winkle who had fallen asleep in 1965 and awakened in 1976 would have observed:

At every turn Rip Van Winkle would encounter lamentations about the failure of all national efforts to reduce inequality and eliminate poverty, to improve schools, to reduce unemployment and its hardships; he would find a sense that not only had past efforts failed, but future ones were also doomed by the incapacity of government to act effectively.[10]

What went wrong after 1965? Extensive evaluation research was conducted by the congressional staff—whose size had tripled to about 20,000 over the past quarter century—by the Legislative Reference Service of the Library of Congress, the General Accounting Office, the Office of Management and Budget, the Department of HEW and by numerous academic, nonprofit or commercial research outfits, usually on a contract basis. Most of their findings were from guarded to negative; a few tried to be as hopeful as facts would permit them to be.

But Congress paid limited attention to the researchers' conclusions.

14

Debates on extension and enlargement of programs tended to focus mainly on the share of federal money each member's district or state was scheduled to receive. Committee and floor fights centered on how to split the pie.

Still, the failure of the 1960s programs to produce what their sponsors had promised, contributed to the defeat of more extensive proposals in the three major social fields: welfare, education and health. Plans to authorize a guaranteed annual income, general aid to public schools and colleges, comprehensive national health insurance, though intensely lobbied for over many years were never enacted. They may now have a great future behind them.

Henry Aaron suggested in his above quoted book that most of the social programs were not based on research findings but on preconceived notions. They were founded on how the programs' authors *thought* people are and ought to act, not on how people really are. Bitter and costly experience showed that problems such as poverty, inadequate learning, low or no occupational skills, misbehavior toward themselves, others and society as a whole, are more complicated than was thought and far more difficult to remedy than most had believed.

Some social or economic problems can be resolved or alleviated by proper methods but some cannot, even by huge amounts of public money, given unfortunate limitations to the malleability of the human mind. Too often, minor problems are turned into major ones by well-intentioned but quixotic governmental attempts at simple solutions by trying to change the traits and behavior of human beings. This became increasingly evident in the 1970s and disillusion supplanted earlier hopes. *Common Cause* wrote in 1980: "The reason the United States Government cannot solve the urgent problems that are plaguing our country, is because *the government is the problem*."[11] The escapades of the welfare state in the 1960s caused many problems for the United States to arise, many minor problems to become serious.

The word welfare itself gradually acquired an ominous reputation. When in 1979 education was raised to cabinet rank, the Department of HEW of which it had been a part for 26 years was under the original bill to be renamed Department of Health and Welfare. But because the term "welfare" had become a term of scorn, Congress decided not to burden the new department with such a title and baptized it Department of Health and Human Services.

With enormous sums poured into hundreds of social welfare

programs—totaling $350 billion in 1978—tangible and significant progress was widely expected. Some advances were in fact achieved. The incidence of income inadequacy was sharply reduced to a point where only minor pockets of poverty remained. The War on Poverty succeeded. But not as its protagonists had said it would, by making poor people self-supporting, by training and helping them to become contributing members of society, by shifting "from welfare to workfare." The size of the poverty population was reduced by handing out larger benefits to more people, by making increasing numbers perpetually welfare-dependent. Widespread poverty, Congress was told, was at the root of most social ills which could be sharply reduced by lifting more people above the poverty threshold. This could be done by multiplying funds for the schools, for occupational training and various forms of assistance to disadvantaged people, by removing obstacles to equal opportunity.

Unfortunately it did not work. Property crime, delinquency, family breakdown, illegitimacy and other types of social ills, new and old, have been increasing at a frightening rate. While the number of persons below the poverty line dropped sharply, the number of property crimes (robbery, burglary, auto theft, etc.) reported by the FBI jumped from 2.4 million in 1964 to 5.1 million in 1972, to 11 million in 1979.

The income and outcome of education have been moving in opposite directions. Expenditures for public education per student tripled in *constant* dollars while measurable results in terms of skills and knowledge went down steadily. Educational institutions have been the breeding places of crime, civic strife, and contempt of law. That is why schools and colleges no longer rank as high in the respect and affection of the American people as they did throughout most of our history.

Urban conflagrations indicate that deep-seated unhappiness, frustration, and hatred characterize wide sections of our people. One of the ugliest pages in American history was being written just as the welfare state was put into practice. Our worst series of street riots began shortly after the passage of the Economic Opportunity Act of 1964. A succession of campus rebellions began soon after Congress passed several laws providing institutional and student aid and colleges began actively recruiting and admitting students who were below established standards. Our worst urban fights over the schools followed the expansion of compensatory education. Perhaps we can trace this widespread bitterness and upheaval to false hopes raised beyond any possibility of fulfillment and bound to be disappointed. We may now be seeing the results of acting as if all social ills could be cured by generous infusions of public money, of pretending that the effect of a law will be what its preamble says it should be.

Attempts to correlate tangible achievements with the resources applied to a program have cast great doubt on the idea that improvements are necessarily proportionate to the amounts spent or even tend to be favorably affected. In case after case we must question whether there is a positive cost-quality relationship or whether expenditures have been counterproductive. Huge federal spending has not brought forth social miracles, but has instead created resentment among those who felt cheated when the promised results failed to materialize as the money was dissipated.

We are increasingly offering people perverse incentives, especially through our welfare and tax systems. By making workless benefits often more attractive to unskilled people than laboring at menial jobs, by stiffening tax penalties for working harder and succeeding, by making it financially more attractive to some families to have its breadwinner abandon it, by making it taxwise profitable for some to seek a divorce, by demonstrating that the promises of government and its leaders cannot be trusted and that each individual had better look out for himself by any means and that crime often does pay, we continually strengthen destructive trends in our society.

Why are the facts not brought out more clearly for the public? A major reason is that the specialists in the various areas of social welfare, and particularly the best known among them, are committed to expanded federal spending for the goals of their professional and special interest organizations. Those are the experts that are called in and relied on by government agencies, by some of the major foundations, and by the nation's leading press. Young graduates in the social sciences soon learn on which side the bread is buttered. They find out that good jobs, grants, and publicity go to the enthusiasts for enlarged federal spending, while the critics have a hard row to hoe. Small wonder that so many of our young people devise their strategies accordingly.

The Great Society programs made substantial progress toward their proclaimed primary aim: to eliminate poverty. Applying the official poverty threshold—cash income of $7450 for a family of four in 1979—the percentage of persons below that standard dropped from about 22% of the total population in the early 1960s to 11.6% in 1979. Considering *in-kind* income such as food stamps, housing subsidies, child nutrition, medical services, etc., the incidence of poverty is probably half the official rate, that is, somewhere between 5% and 6%. Since some people are in a low economic bracket only temporarily or by choice, the United States is probably as close to a minimum incidence of poverty as seems currently practicable. Spending for poverty programs, however, continues up because of growth factors built into the statutory formulas which are not subject to control by the budgetary process.

The primary drive of the welfare state, as it has developed in recent decades, aims at ever greater income redistribution toward an egalitarian ideal. It has misdirected attention from efforts to bake a bigger pie to fighting over the division of the pie. Often it has put persons in charge who don't know how to bake a bigger or better pie nor care. They mainly focus on their own slice.

A lopsided and discriminatory tax system has reduced incentives and thereby work efforts as well as capital formation and productive investment. This, in turn, resulted in a shrinking rate of productivity growth—which turned negative in the late 1970s and a standstill in the growth of real (*constant* $) per capita income.

One consequence of the continuing rapid increase in domestic expenditure, exceeding the growth rate of governmental revenue, is a huge budgetary deficit, year after year, which is a major force in keeping inflation rates at high levels. The adverse impact of large welfare outlays on the availability of funds for an adequate defense was mentioned earlier.

In summary: excesses of the welfare state in the past three decades have produced a poor harvest, indeed.

How Secure is Social Security?

The three governmental activities whose outlays in 1978 aggregated nearly twice as much as all other public domestic spending combined—and which also grew faster than the rest—were income support, education and medical care.

At $157 billion (federal-state-local) in 1978, income support is the largest and most rapidly expanding function. It comprises old age and survivors insurance (OASI) at $81 billion, disability insurance (DI) at

$12 billion, public assistance and related welfare programs at $55 billion, and unemployment compensation at $9 billion.

OASI, better known as social security, is the biggest of these programs. Over 100 million workers—more than 90% of all working persons—now participate and contribute—government employees being the largest excluded group—and over 30 million persons receive benefits. As one of the New Deal's most successful creations, social security is firmly established as the nations' largest intergenerational transfer program—from the productive to the no-longer-working population. Its security, resting on the universal support and confidence of its members, would not even be questioned were it not for recurring financial crises, caused by Congress' irrepressible tendency to boost benefits at a faster rate than taxes. Not that taxes had not been raised. Social security tax rates multiplied fourfold over the past quarter century and tax collections six times faster than covered earnings.

Social security combines two systems into an uneasy conglomerate: a) insurance against loss of earnings due to retirement in return for premiums paid by the worker and his employer; b) welfare payments to persons who for whatever reason did not accumulate enough credits by contributions to give them an annuity high enough to sustain them in their later years.

To satisfy the welfare requirements, eligibility provisions have been enormously liberalized, benefits are heavily skewed in favor of persons with low earnings records and benefits are annually escalated by the consumer price index (CPI).

That adds up to a politically highly successful formula for drawing support to a program whose workings and intricate contribution-benefit formulas virtually no one can understand. It makes social security an effective income redistribution machine not only between generations but also from higher to lower income persons, without its involuntary benefactors ever knowing about it. But it also causes major economic problems which would have bankrupted an insurance company long ago.

The social security tax increase effective in 1979—the nation's biggest tax boost ever and among its most clever soak-the-rich schemes—was supposed to assure the system's liquidity for decades. As it now appears, the social security trust fund may run dry by 1982 or 1983 unless something is done about it.

Something will, most assuredly, be done about it. No government, no Congress could survive a default of social security, now or ever. Tax rates could be raised further—they still are below most European social security tax rates. Tapping other sources has been much talked about but is unlikely to happen, at least as long as the government's general fund runs heavily in the red. A value-added tax will certainly be imposed in the United States—someday. But that day is not now nor will be until a major national emergency arises. It won't be done just for social security. A shift of funds from disability to social security helped temporarily, but is only a short-lived expedient.

The long-range solution is a slimming down of benefits which have grown beyond any justification. Congress has forbidden mandatory retirement before age 70. But more workers now apply for retirement benefits at ages 62 to 64 than at age 65. The penalty for early receipt is too small as is the bonus for deferring receipt. Standard age for receipt will have to be gradually pushed up to 68. That does not have to be done now. It could be postponed until after the turn of the century when the contributor-beneficiary ratio shrinks from 3:1 to 2:1. Starting it soon, say at the rate of one month postponement each year, would make the adjustment far smoother.

To continue escalating income by the CPI is a surefire prescription for continuing inflation indefinitely. Many wage rates now escalate at rates lower than the CPI and social security pensions may have to follow suit. Some types of benefits will have to be cut or eliminated.

The average monthly benefit of a retired worker or his family multiplied 2.5 times in *constant* dollars between 1940 and 1978. That may be overdoing a good thing, considering that most large employers now operate supplemental retirement programs. The governing formula grants recipients in the low brackets 90% of their wage base as benefit, but only 15% for earnings from $1171 a month up. Sweetened by a "grandfather clause" this means that effective June 1980 a worker with a monthly earnings base of $400, retiring at age 65, is entitled to $422.50 a month if alone, to $633.30 if married; if he dies, his widow and one child will receive $738.90.[12]

That benefit formula makes social security retirement not too hard to bear. Whether the generation of workers paying for it—one-half by deductions, one-half through higher prices—will find the steadily increasing cost as easy to bear, remains to be seen. Some reforms in the benefit structure are overdue. Many working women get little or no return on their contributions. Many men get less over their remaining lifetime than women with the same contributions record to their credit. Could there be a fair adjustment on both sides?

It has been proposed that social security benefits should be taxable as income, as they are in some European countries. In the United States, the difference between a worker's contributions to a *nongovernmental* retirement system and his subsequent receipts are taxable. Would it not seem fair to tax half the social security receipts as income, since half the contributions are paid by the employer? If Congress made social security payments taxable, it would be under heavy pressure to raise benefits of most recipients commensurately. That would make net savings to the government minimal.

Public Welfare in the Welfare State

Social insurance programs, though they contain a substantial welfare element, do not reach all needy persons. That is why the *Social Security Act of 1935* established several public assistance programs to aid persons who for tangible and demonstrable reasons are unable to provide for their own sustenance. It was generally assumed at the time, and for many years later, that social insurance programs, as they matured and achieved universal coverage, would gradually absorb most public assistance recipients so that special programs for them would no longer be necessary or, at least, would shrink to minimal size.

Most of the needy persons for whom the early assistance programs were intended did indeed move to social insurance. Aid programs would have diminished had it not been for other groups, not intended by the programs' authors to be eligible for federal assistance, which began to move in during the 1950s and took over within a few years, helped by federal and state administrators. Many new forms of assistance came into being. Public welfare programs in cash, in kind, in subsidies, in a great variety of services virtually exploded, as the welfare state reached its maturity in succeeding decades.

There are now hundreds of such programs whose outlays in 1978 totaled $55 billion (excluding medical, housing, veterans benefits) up from $3 billion in 1952.[13] In 1979 one-third of American households were receiving in-kind (noncash) aid. More than half the households in each of the four categories—food, housing, Medicare, Medicaid—had a cash income above the official poverty line, which, beginning July 1, 1981, was set at $8400 for a family of four. Among the biggest of these

21

programs, in terms of beneficiaries, is the *Food Stamp Program* which now reaches more than 20 million persons—nearly one American in ten—who, despite huge income support programs, presumably cannot afford to pay for their food and are given a subsidy which now averages $500 a year. It replaced direct distribution to needy persons of basic food commodities, which never gained much popularity among them and cost less than $100 million a year in the early to mid-1950s. The food stamp program, now at about $10 billion a year, is strongly supported not only by organizations of current and potential recipients but also by agricultural interests, food producers and processors, supermarket chains and grocers. It has become an institution whose supporters have been able to frustrate all attempts at curtailing it or reverting to direct distribution of nutritious food items to those who genuinely need them. The United States may be the only country in history whose lowest income class has a higher incidence of obesity than its middle and upper classes.

But the program that can best illustrate the nature and impact of the welfare state over the past three decades is *Aid to Families With Dependent Children (AFDC)*, with over 10 million recipients at a current annual cost of $13 billion. AFDC has for many years been the most controversial of the welfare programs and would have been abolished long ago if its critics had been able to agree on a replacement. When established in 1935, ADC (as it was then called) was so uncontroversial that it was not even mentioned in the extensive congressional debates on the Social Security Act, except for a few words, stressing that it was needed:

> Death through the loss of the breadwinner, has broken many a home. For centuries the widows, orphans and dependent children have cried aloud for help and assistance in their tragic periods of economic insecurity. In the past the only recourse for orphaned children was the poorhouse, almshouse, and the orphan asylum. . . .

ADC was intended to supplement the states' widows' pensions with federal funds and so did for some years. But as the orphans shifted to social security in the 1940s and 1950s, ADC was perverted into something it was not intended to be: an escape from the necessity to work for a living by low-skilled people who refuse to accept jobs at a skill level they *can* handle, at a wage commensurate with the value of their service.

Over the past thirty years AFDC has become the regular and accepted way of life for over three million women and men—for most of the latter indirectly or surreptitiously—and has widely replaced employment as the normal source of sustenance. It is now the preferred and respected mode of living, blessed with the government's seal of approval, in poverty or slum sections of many American cities. AFDC has become a major nutrient in the breeding grounds of crime, delinquency, illegitimacy, prostitution, and other forms of social ills, for a new generation to repeat and possibly excel in their parents' careers.

In his State of the Union Message in 1935 Franklin D. Roosevelt warned:

> The lessons of history . . . show conclusively. . . that continued dependence upon relief induces a spiritual and moral disintegration fundamentally destructive to the national fibre. To dole out relief is to administer a narcotic, a subtle destroyer of the human spirit. . . .
> The Federal Government must and shall quit this business of relief.

Truer words were never spoken: AFDC has turned into a cancer on society, planted and nursed by the federal government which has been getting deeper and deeper into "this business of relief" in the 4–1/2 decades since Roosevelt's warning.

Between 1952 and 1978 the number of under 18-year-old children in the United States grew by 26%, the number of children on AFDC by 383%. That happened over a period during which the number of jobs grew by 57%—though total population expanded only 39%—while GNP in real terms more than doubled (increase 134%), and per capita disposable income in *constant* dollars, almost doubled (increase 83%). One out of every nine children is now on AFDC. But fewer than 3% of those children are orphans, with a slightly larger number having a disabled parent.

In 1978, 85% of the children on AFDC were on the rolls because their parents would not support them. Nothing like that has ever happened before, anywhere, anytime. Daniel P. Moynihan, now the senior senator from New York, remarked in 1968: "Throughout most of history a man who deserted his children pretty much ensured that they would starve, or near to it, if he was not brought back, and that he would be horsewhipped if he were." Moynihan commented: "The poor of the United States today enjoy a quite unprecedented de facto freedom to abandon their children in the certain knowledge that society will care for them and, what is more, in a state such as New York, to care for them by quite decent standards."[14] In most AFDC cases the fathers are "absent"—a euphemism for having deserted—and the mothers regard their children as a meal ticket to a life of leisure, rather than labor and bring home the bread—as most parents have always done and will always do.

For nearly half a century several presidents of the United States have attempted, in Franklin Roosevelt's words, "to substitute work for relief."

John Kennedy in 1962 submitted, prepared and carried out extensive plans for occupational training and a shift to self-support. So did Lyndon Johnson in 1964 who, on signing the *Economic Opportunity Act of 1964* remarked, "The days of the dole in our country are numbered." Richard Nixon in 1969 wrote, "I propose a new approach that will make it more attractive to go to work than go on welfare. . . ."

Jimmy Carter said in 1977, ". . . I am asking the Congress to abolish our existing welfare system, and replace it with a job-oriented program for those able to work. . . ."

In the same message Mr. Carter criticized the existing program, meaning AFDC:

> The welfare system is anti-work, anti-family, inequitable in its treatment of the poor and wasteful of the taxpayers' dollars. . . . It provides incentives for family breakup. In most cases two-parent families are not eligible for cash assistance and, therefore, a working father often can increase his family's income by leaving home. . . ."

But AFDC is still going strong though it no longer is expanding as it formerly did.

Unfortunately, the replacement for AFDC which Mr. Nixon and Mr. Carter proposed would have gotten us from the frying pan into the fire. Which is why Congress between 1972 and 1979 repeatedly rejected presidential plans for a guaranteed annual income. Not only because of technical difficulties or disagreements over the maximum income that would make a family eligible for assistance, or over the amount of aid and the prospective total cost. Nor over the impossibility of reducing assistance payments to persons who had some work earnings, while maintaining their motivation to seek and keep a job (the problem of the "notches").

The conflict is more basic. Original public assistance programs required proof of need that stemmed from objectively determinable and verifiable causes, which are not readily subject to manipulation, such as old age, blindness, disability, death or incapacity of the breadwinner. Low actual or potential earnings or income are not an adequate criterion for assistance eligibility because there are millions of persons who will settle for small but easily obtainable income if it enables them to avoid work. For many persons a frugal life and leisure beat toiling in the sweat of their brow.

I told the Senate Finance Committee, considering President Nixon's version of a guaranteed annual income on January 27, 1972 (after I had left the White House staff):

> A national system of public assistance that disregards the causes of dependence and offers benefits comparable to low-skill wages is bound to grow without limit. It is a permanent and irresistible invitation to abuse and ruin. In most AFDC cases the cause of need is not economic but social and requires individual consideration and judgment which are impossible under a national uniform program.

Extensive manpower training programs, costing billions of dollars, have had scant success. There are unskilled and low-skilled job openings around galore—but why should welfare recipients take them? Poor people may often be of low intelligence, but they are not stupid. Why should they work? Hundreds of thousands of low-skilled jobs are going begging in state employment offices. Metropolitan newspapers carry many pages of "help wanted" advertising. Proposals of stricter enforcement of laws against illegal immigration are strongly opposed by employers who are unable to attract enough Americans to unskilled and often menial and low-paid jobs. The New York subway is filthy, household garbage is being collected at long and irregular intervals and left in alleys and streets in some sections of the city, parks are neglected and certain areas filled with refuse, rubble, and decay. But to expect welfare recipients to help clean up the city or at least their own neighborhoods, or work as domestics, would be deemed an indignity.

It is interesting to contemplate how clean the subways, streets, and parks are in Moscow and Leningrad—with whole swarms of men and women cleaning them all the time. But then, the Soviet Union offers no welfare or unemployment pay to ablebodied persons and its minimum monthly wage equals only $100. Ours went to $580, based on a 40 hour week, on January 1, 1981. The Soviet constitution prescribes that: "He who does not work, neither shall he eat." In the United States that principle of Saint Paul has long yielded to the welfare state precept that ties between work and income should be weakened and eventually cut. We practice the first part of the Soviet rule, "from each according to his ability, to each according to his work," but we would not think of practicing the second part. Soviet citizens are guaranteed the right to work. Would the United States not be better off if it guaranteed everybody an *opportunity to earn* a living instead of accepting the principle that the government *owes everybody a living*?

When Governor Reagan of California established a work requirement for AFDC in 1971—and had enough political pull in Washington to get a temporary exemption from the federal ban on work relief—AFDC rolls dropped by 342,000 between March 1971 and June 1974. The number of AFDC recipients declined in California by 21% while simultaneously they nationally increased by 6%. The reform, in the words of Reagan's welfare administrator Charles D. Hobbs, made welfare "an unattractive alternative to work for ablebodied recipients."

How can the problem of AFDC, and of public assistance in general, be resolved?

1. Both parents, if ablebodied, should be held responsible for the support of their children.

2. Refusal to accept a job because it is "menial," "unsuitable," cumbersome, low-paid should make a person ineligible for any type of public aid.

3. Parents who claim to be unable to find a job, and cannot be referred to an opening by the state employment service, should have to perform government-assigned work, with most of their compensation, except for an austere minimum, withheld to pay for the cost of maintaining their children.

4. Failure to support one's children, except for compelling and demonstrable reasons, should be made a federal offense for both parents.

5. Public assistance should be a local, not a federal, responsibility. This does not exclude federal financial assistance through block grants to states for distribution to local jurisdictions, with amounts based on objective formulas taking relevant facts into consideration (closed-end appropriations).

6. Decisions on whether parents should be required to work—or be partially or wholly exempted because of personal impairment—require individual judgment in each case which can be properly exercised only under local control because no nationally uniform system can do justice to the infinite variety of types of need, individual problems and potentials. Communities should be able to decide on the standards at which they wish to support their needy members.

Aid to the Unemployed or to Unemployment?

Unemployment in an industrial society is an economic problem, but even more so, a human and political problem. In recent decades rising unemployment rates have generally been regarded as an indication that the private economy was unable to generate enough job openings because of inadequate effective consumer purchasing power and demand. The standard therapy has been for government to pump more money into the bloodstream so as to boost the ability of consumers and business firms to enlarge their buying. Perpetual inflation has been the inevitable result of this policy which only in the past few years has come under some doubt among government policymakers.

The official unemployment rate is outright misleading. It doubled between 1952 and 1978 from 3.0% to 6.0%. Over the same time span, the working age population increased 48%, the number of persons holding civilian jobs 57%, but the number of those who reported themselves unemployed by 212%. The employment-to-population ratio has steadily improved while the official unemployment rate has worsened. The number of overtime hours has consistently equaled a greater percentage of all hours worked than the official unemployment rate. Moonlighting, i.e., multiple job holding, is reported at about 5%, the number of help-wanted ads has been increasing. Much of the opposition to a stricter enforcement of immigration laws—whose lax administration now enables five or more million illegal immigrants to remain and keep jobs here, with the number steadily growing—comes

27

from employers who insist that they would be unable to obtain enough workers to fill unskilled, menial, low-paid vacancies if the flow from south of the border were curtailed. If those immigrants are able to find jobs, why can't Americans?

Only about one-third of the unemployed actually lost their last job; most quit, were would-be new entrants to the labor market, or were on temporary layoffs. Why is it that the unemployment rate is consistently 2-1/2 to 4 times higher for single men than for family men? Few companies are likely to discriminate against applicants because they are not married. But the man with family responsibilities is less likely to quit a post until he has another and, if he loses his job, will be pounding the streets the next morning. A single man may not mind taking some time off for fishing—after telling his boss where to go if he did not like it.

Unemployment compensation is an essential program in an industrial society to avoid or alleviate severe hardship, misery and, sometimes, tragedy. Weekly benefits of skilled and highly paid workers equal less than 50%, 40% or even 30% than their prior *net* take-home pay (that is, after deducting work-related expenses). But millions of unskilled workers are now entitled to 60% or more of what they are able to earn on the type of opening for which they are qualified. What incentive do they have to labor at menial and cumbersome chores for a just a few dollars more than the dole—except for the time it takes to acquire enough credits?

Three-fourths of the unemployed have been jobless for less than 15 weeks, only 13% for over 26 weeks. That may relate to state unemployment laws which generally limit benefit entitlement to 26 weeks. The federal government, however, subsidizes another 13 weeks of benefits and at times up to 65 weeks.

To cut off unemployment compensation at any time is a painful and sometimes wrenching action. There are sizable numbers of men and women who for reasons of personal inadequacy or local economic conditions may have to make severe adjustments to qualify for another job. It may take time to realize that they can't do better than what is available. Unemployment compensation beneficiaries are supposed to accept a "suitable" job—a term that can be and widely is interpreted as meaning a job of the type, at the level, compensation, and location the individual was accustomed to. The "suitable" job provision may have to be changed to "any" job, after a period of several weeks.

Instead of cutting off unemployment benefits at a particular point,

28

which in many cases may amount to severe deprivation, it might be preferable to gradually reduce the amount every few weeks—after an initial period. That would put the recipient on notice that his time is running out and that economic pressure will continue to increase until he is ready to make certain unpleasant but necessary personal adjustments.

The widening of employment opportunities is limited by counter-productive provisions in our tax laws and business regulations. Industrial and job expansion requires large capital investments which are discouraged by punitive taxation. It may be politically profitable to reduce taxes for millions of persons in the below-average income brackets and offset the revenue loss by keeping business taxes high or even boosting them. That is always good for getting more votes. But it also explains why savings, capital formation, industrial investment rates are lower in the United States than in most other industrial countries.

Through organized union pressure with government assistance, some wages—legal minimum or contractual rates—in the United States have been pushed to levels where the products of our labor are no longer internationally competitive. That is why some operations have been shifted abroad, and why imports sometimes look pricewise more attractive. American factories could sell more automobiles and numerous other products if they could be offered, here and abroad, at prices that make them more desirable than the output of their foreign competitors.

Easy availability and generosity of unemployment benefits was bound sooner or later to get the system into trouble. In the mid-1970s some of the states' trust funds ran dry and half of them had to borrow large sums from the United States Treasury to be able to continue writing compensation checks. Less than one-third of those advances was repaid in subsequent years and 15 states still owe large amounts. To investigate the system's health, Congress in 1976 established a National Commission on Unemployment Compensation which reported in June 1980 that benefits had exceeded revenues by $12.9 billion between 1970 and 1979, that federal trust funds were $12.8 billion in debt, and concluded in its final report that "there is reason to question whether the unemployment insurance system can recover financially, given current funding provisions at both the state and federal levels." The commission submitted recommendations which, with several dissents, tended, on balance, to enlarge benefit payments substantially. It proposed to increase the federal taxable wage base, to cancel past debts, and to shift financial responsibility for the federal-state system further to the national government.

Those recommendations would not restore solvency to the system. The Department of Labor estimated in July 1980 that state trust funds might have to borrow another $18 billion between 1980 and 1985 to keep paying compensation claims. This would be another step in the federalization of unemployment insurance which some organizations have long been demanding.

An alternative would be to leave responsibility for unemployment compensation to the states, save under emergency conditions. State legislatures would then be faced with the alternative of keeping benefits under control or raising taxes to a level which could adversely affect the state's ability to compete for industrial location.

The Income and the Outcome of Education

Americans have always viewed and treated education with special affection and, for much of history, had reason to be proud of the excellence of their educational institutions. They know that a good part of the enormous progress which our civilization has achieved can be attributed to a tireless effort and huge investment in schools and colleges. Educational outlays in the U.S. are now estimated at $200 billion a year, equal to 7.5% of GNP, compared with 4.1% of GNP in the USSR. With about 30% of America's population involved—59 million as students, 6.6 million as employees, education—depending on what yardstick we use—may be the country's biggest industry.

As in most countries, our educational system is largely a governmental enterprise, with 90% of enrollment at elementary-secondary levels and 78% at the college and university level in publicly owned and operated institutions. But very little of this is federal; most of it is state, local or private. The national government has for the past dozen years been providing about ten percent of the income of schools and colleges, largely for special programs. About ninety percent of the institutions' revenues are raised through state and local taxes, tuitions and voluntary contributions.

Our most successful men and women, the leaders in most fields, are generally well educated, though some are self-educated. Our least successful people, those with the smallest earnings, tend to rank low in educational achievements, are deficient in basic skills, and have

30

attended school for fewer years than those higher up on the socio-economic ladder.

This has led many to seek the cause of income differences among people in the number of years they attended school and in the amount of money that was spent on their respective schools. It has long been customary to measure educational quality in dollars spent per pupil, in the teacher-pupil ratio, and similar measures of *input*. Complaints about deficiencies in the *output*, the products of education, were answered with the same plea: give us more money, hire more teachers and pay them more. The American people did. Here is what has happened since the early 1950s:

PUBLIC SCHOOLS AND COLLEGES, 1952 and 1978

	1952	1978	Percent Increase
Students in public education	27,862,000	52,818,000	90%
Employees in public education	1,884,000	6,586,000	250
Expenditure for public education			
current $	$8.4 billion	$120.8 billion	1338
1978 $	20.6 billion	120.8 billion	486
Number of students per employee	14.8	8.0	−46
Expenditure per student			
current $	$ 301	$2288	660
1978 $	740	2288	209

SOURCES: U.S. Department of Commerce, Bureau of Economic Analysis, *The National Income and Product Accounts of the United States, 1929–1974*, a Supplement to the *Survey of Current Business*, 1977; idem, *Survey of Current Business, National Income Issue*, July 1979; U.S. Bureau of the Census, *Historical Statistics on Governmental Finances and Employment*, 1967 Census of Governments, 1969; and idem, *Public Employment in 1978*, 1979; U.S. Office of Education, *Statistical Summary of Education, 1951–52*, 1955; and National Center for Education Statistics, *Digest of Education Statistics, 1979*, 1979.

The table above should, once and for all, kill the myth of American schools being underfed or starving.

Financial support (in *constant* dollars) and staff multiplied 2 to 3 times faster than students over the past quarter century. UNESCO reported that in 1975 public expenditure on education per inhabitant was in North America more than twice as high as in Europe and more than three times higher than in the Soviet Union. But there are no indications that those differing levels of spending are even remotely reflected in the students' learning.

Some of our major urban public school systems—Cleveland, Chicago, New York—are reported to be in financial trouble. Boston's public schools revealed in April 1981 that they had exhausted their $210 million appropriation and would have to close unless another $38 million were forthcoming. Why is $3256 per student not enough? Why do Boston schools need $3845 for each of their students? Because they employ 5,000 teachers and a total staff of 11,000 for 64,500 students. Do Boston schools really need one teacher for every 12.9 students, one employee for every 5.9 students? This is the crux of the problem.

The evidence is overwhelming that there is little, if any, cost-quality relationship in the schools. Johns Hopkins sociologist James

Figure 4
RATE OF INCREASE IN STUDENTS AND EMPLOYEES IN PUBLIC EDUCATION
1952 to 1978

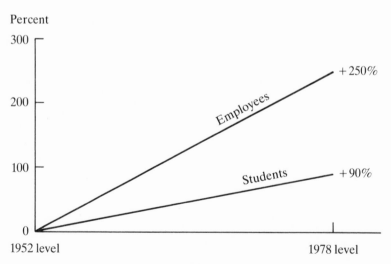

Coleman so found to his surprise, and concluded after completing the most extensive government-sponsored study of American schools ever undertaken (*Equality of Educational Opportunity, 1966*) that "the evidence revealed that within broad geographic regions, and for each racial and ethnic group, the physical and economic resources going into a school has very little relationship to the achievements coming out of it." Harvard's Christopher Jencks, in summarizing the ensuing national debate, concluded: "Variations in schools' fiscal and human resources have very little effect on student achievement—probably even less than the Coleman Report implied." Hundreds of class-size studies show that students do not learn more in smaller classes.

While expenditures per pupil were increasing every year and the number of pupils per class was shrinking, learning achievements in the schools were falling: mean scores on college board tests (SAT's), have been declining dramatically for nearly two decades, from 478 (verbal) and 502 (mathematical)—out of a possible 800—in 1962, to 424 and 466 respectively in 1980. What may be even more ominous: the number of students with high verbal scores, 650 or above, fell from 53,794 in 1972 to 29,019 in 1980. This means that knowledge and skills even among our most gifted students—upon whom the nation's future depends—are deteriorating because they are not faced with a sufficiently exacting curriculum nor with high standards of grading and graduation.

High school test scores in mathematics, writing, science, etc., have been dropping over the past ten years, according to studies of the National Assessment of Educational Progress.

That may help explain the recent deterioration in general regard, as reported in annual Gallup polls of public attitudes toward the public schools. "A" ratings of the schools dropped to nearly half between 1974 and 1980, "D" or fail ratings almost doubled.

In 1965, Congress was persuaded that a vast expansion of "compensatory education" programs would reduce the lag of one or several years in basic skills of children from low-income backgrounds. Now, fifteen years and thirty billion dollars later, the record of projects, from "Higher Horizons" and "More Effective Schools" in New York to "Bannecker" in St. Louis, from "Madison" in Syracuse to the Berkeley schools, and of tens of thousands of projects under Title I, all of them begun with great enthusiasm, tell a story of consistent failure to produce the educational improvement among so-called deprived children that their sponsors had hoped for and promised.

In his school reform message of March 3, 1970, President Richard M. Nixon reported that "the best available evidence indicates that most of the compensatory education programs have not measurably helped poor children catch up. . . . In our Headstart program, where so much hope is invested, we find that youngsters enrolled only for the summer achieve almost no gains, and the gains of those in the program for a full year are soon matched by their non-Headstart classmates from similar poor backgrounds." Several subsequent reports, with a few exceptions, have confirmed these findings.

These efforts at compensatory education resemble nothing as much as the quest of the alchemists who, for hundreds of years and at a huge cost, tried to accomplish what we now know cannot be done.

Our gifted children are, on graduation from public high school, an average of two years behind their counterparts in European secondary schools. Less endowed children, on leaving the schools, with or without a diploma, lack essential knowledge and vital marketable skills. That is one reason why so many of our young people are unable to land or keep jobs, why so many drift aimlessly from one casual post to another.

Why are the American people getting less education for more dollars? What are the schools doing wrong? Some try to explain the appalling outcome as a consequence of the near monopoly position of the public schools: there is almost no competition that would offer a higher quality education. Thus schools have sunk to the lowest common denominator. That sounds reasonable but is no adequate explanation. Public education enjoys even more of a monopoly position in most European countries. But the graduates of their secondary schools are upon graduation, as mentioned above, ahead of ours, either academically or in their readiness to fill nonacademic jobs.

A major reason for the failure of learning is the frightful lack of discipline which our school administrators have allowed to grow worse, year after year. The existence of the "blackboard jungle" has long been known. But the multiplication of outright crimes—personal assaults and property offenses—against teachers and fellow students, of vandalism to buildings and equipment, have been continuing without effective counteraction. New York City's Board of Education reported in 1980 that school crimes had increased 150 percent since 1975 and were still soaring.

Permissiveness has increasingly characterized public school policy. It is yielding a bitter harvest. Administrators are reluctant to impose

34

severe enough punishment, whether in school or through criminal prosecution, and often dare not act for fear of personal reprisals. Federal agencies and courts have outrageously interfered with attempts by courageous principals, trying to enforce civilized behavior in their schools. No other country would tolerate the chaotic conditions which characterize many of our urban schools.

The officially recommended softness toward offenders of essential rules of civil behavior, the eagerness to overlook and excuse transgressions, only encourages more violence. It is the philosophy of a welfare state gone astray which allows individuals to blame their frustrations and inadequacies on "the system" and enables them to vent their wrath on innocent victims and on the representatives of what they view as oppressive authority.

It is now hard to remember that the school systems of major American cities were once famed for their educational eminence. There is no hope of even beginning to restore learning to its former level without first restoring firm discipline. No compromise has a chance of success.

What else can be and needs to be done to uplift the quality of education in our schools? For many years, curriculum content has been allowed to sink to ever lower levels and standards were widely abandoned. To a large extent this can be traced to federal influence. As federal agencies exerted increasing control over the policies and practices of educational institutions, the power of elected or appointed boards diminished. Schools are now overregulated. Only by restoring to local authorities effective control, without federal interference, can they be enabled to raise educational quality.

For too many years, students have been permitted to choose "breeze" courses in preference to hard subjects, have been able to advance and get a diploma without mastery of essential subject matter. Standards of grading, promotion and graduation must be brought up at least to where they once were. This would motivate students with sufficient intellectual capacity and aspiration to develop their skills and knowledge so that upon graduation from secondary school their achievements would be comparable to those of their European counterparts.

We know that it would be nonsense to have all people jump hurdles of the same height. Whatever uniform height we chose would be too high for some, too low for others. Why do we believe that what does not work in an athletic pursuit will work in an intellectual pursuit? If

35

all children are to develop their individual capacities to the fullest, each must be faced with a task that requires his best effort, whether his capacity be high or low.

We are now using hurdles in school which are too low for gifted children. But to upgrade the curriculum, to raise to higher levels standards of grading, promotion, graduation, would cause children of lesser endowment to fall even further behind. They would be discouraged, feel more frustrated than they are now. Unable to cope, they would drop out of school with an even more inadequate preparation for their life's work.

This is why suggestions to require minimum competency testing for grade promotion or graduation—which several states are considering or have instituted—have run into such fierce opposition. Low as standards now are in American public schools, and essential as higher standards are if the quality of education is to be improved, the imposition of elevated standards would be disastrous for millions of children who cannot absorb and assimilate a curriculum of rigorous intellectual content.

Under our current system, gifted children tend to goldbrick, when they find out that they can get by with little or no effort. Many others despair and give up when faced by demands beyond their capacity. We now find that, for example, an 8th grade class may have students who perform at 10th or 11th grade level, and others who manage the 3 Rs at 4th or 5th grade level. No teacher can do justice to all or a majority of them, no matter how small the class size.

How do countries outside the United States manage to educate children of widely differing ability? None are trying to educate all children up to age 18 in the same school and in the same classroom. Most countries operate dual or multiple school systems with curricula and standards that enable teachers to face children of differing capacity with tasks they are able to handle.

Three or four parallel tracks or streams are used in some American high schools. But it is done with reluctance, unobtrusively, almost clandestinely, and often with a feeling of embarrassment. Some judges have, in fact, declared parallel tracks to be unconstitutional, in an almost unbelievable misunderstanding of the meaning and intent of the United States Constitution.

Some believe the operation of parallel tracks to violate democratic principles. All human beings are held to be created equal. But they are not, never were, never can be, equal in their individual capacities.

36

Only a school system with several curricula and standards to fit the needs of children at various levels of endowment can develop the students' individual capacities to their fullest.

This seems to violate the egalitarian principle of a welfare state gone wild, of a system which misunderstands what a welfare state is all about: to aid those who meet with misfortune, not to try to make all alike. Procrustes adjusted all his involuntary guests to a uniform length, by stretching some, chopping off the legs of others. That is what our public schools are trying to do intellectually to their students, with inevitably disastrous results.

Some parents attempt to escape from this despotism by sending their children to a private school, not bound by the rules of an educational bureaucracy removed from reality. But the cost of paying twice for education—through school taxes and again through tuition to a private school—is more than most parents can afford. Yet, a diversity of types of schools, to fit a wide range of aspirations, interests, beliefs and abilities is a more effective system than one based on Procrustean principles.

Some have suggested that parents could be given a choice, less dictated by their financial means, by the issuance of government vouchers which can be redeemed at any school, public or private. Others believe that a grant of income tax credits for tuitions (and donations) to private schools constitutes a less radical and more acceptable method. Both proposals offer parents an escape from public school tyranny.

The debasement of educational quality in our schools has reached alarming proportions and must be reversed by drastic reforms if new generations are to be able to maintain American leadership in the free world, and to assure survival of the nation.

The Rockefeller Foundation's report *The Humanities in American Life* in October 1980 concluded that "a dramatic improvement in the quality" of elementary and secondary schools should be made America's top educational priority. It is there, in grade schools and high schools, that a foundation must be laid upon which an education able to cope with the demands of the twenty-first century must be built.

The high schools' failure to transmit to their students essential skills and knowledge has led many colleges and universities to ease their entrance requirements. About one-fourth of freshman classes lack the necessary preparation and must take "bonehead" English or math. But a college is not the proper place to acquire a high school education and far too costly for it. The lowering of standards of admission, curriculum content, and graduation has helped to triple enrollment and degrees over the past quarter century, to a point where now two to three times as high a proportion of our young people attend institutions of higher learning as do their counterparts in Europe's leading countries. But many of those students are only marginally qualified, if at all, and much of what goes on in our colleges and universities can no longer truly be called "higher" education. That is why a big percentage of our college graduates find that they must settle for occupations and positions for which a proper high school education would have sufficed, and why large numbers of degree holders frantically search for jobs which do not exist or for which they are not qualified.

This amounts to an enormous waste of scarce resources—faculty and facilities—and to a squandering of hard-earned family savings, huge amounts of student aid and several years of the young person's time—in the pursuit of a sheepskin which parents and students mistakenly believe to be a passport to a secure and well-paid career and to higher social status.

The egalitarian spirit has driven out the search for excellence in many of our academic institutions. It can be restored only by greater selectivity in admissions, based on objective criteria, a more demanding curriculum and higher standards for the award of degrees. Financial aid should be granted only to manifestly talented applicants who hold a real promise of high achievements, as was the practice until a few decades ago. Many who now vainly try to acquire a higher education, but not truly succeed in a meaningful sense, will be better off and happier in subprofessional or technical occupations in fields in which the number of openings are increasing.

Government Medical Care

Among the three giants of government social services—income support, education and medical care—the last named is the smallest. It also is the only one among them in which public sources bear less than half the cost and the latest in which government assumed a significant role. Prior to the mid-1960s public medical expenditures—excluding Department of Defense and the Veterans Administration—were minor, consisting mostly of the cost of state and local charity hospitals. Americans spent in 1978 $192 billion on medical services of one kind or another, equal to 9% of GNP; 41% of the total was channeled through government.

Rapid expansion of insurance coverage, public and private, was a major factor in the enormous growth of medical costs. Nearly 70% of medical bills are now paid by *third parties* and not by the patient or his family directly, which removes, or at least weakens, cost considerations on the part of the consumer. Much or all of the services seem to come for free. The consumer, of course, bears the cost of the insurance eventually, but most of it unknowingly. It is either withheld from his wages or, if paid by his employer, passed on to the general public in the form of higher prices.

On first glance it appears that the exponential growth of medical spending has paid off. Age-old scourges of mankind such as smallpox, polio, tuberculosis, measles, and typhoid have been wiped out, the incidence or severity of other afflictions sharply reduced. Death rates have been shrinking, ever so slowly, and life expectancies are lengthening, for women more than for men because of significant progress in overcoming the risks of childbirth and related conditions.

But most of the improvements don't come from where most of the money goes. Reduced incidence of major illnesses results mostly from medical research which gets only two cents of the medical dollar. Some once calamitous contagious diseases have been minimized by cleaner sanitary conditions more than by new therapies. Improved dietary habits, the enormous popularity of regular physical exercise, decline in tobacco consumption and greater awareness of the potential of prevention and self-care can claim a good share of the credit. So can the drop in traffic fatalities, the 3rd or 4th largest cause of death.

Most of the medical outlays are allocated to diagnosis and treatment of the sick, by trying to cure diseases or making their symptoms more tolerable. Because those often are painful, disabling or life-threatening emergencies or traumas, they attract more intense attention of patients and their families than less sensational preventative or environmental influences and actions though their provable contribution could be less significant.

Major federal involvement in health care began with the enactment in 1965 of *Medicare*—mostly for persons 65 and over—and *Medicaid* for the indigent, largely persons on public assistance and other social welfare programs. Medicare and Medicaid now account for two-thirds of all public medical outlays. They are firmly established in principle though their approaches and methods, their impact and results, their advantage over alternative avenues to similar goals, remain controversial.

The cost of medical care has risen much faster than other costs. Taking 1952 as 100, the consumer price index (CPI) stood in August 1980 at 314, its medical component at 453. Hospital charges were the leading factor in the rapid rise. Just between 1966 and 1978 the average daily hospital room charge multipled fivefold—from $44 to $225—while the CPI merely doubled. One reason for the disproportionate growth: hospital staffs multiplied threefold between 1952 and 1978 while the number of patient days dropped 19%. More intensive care is now provided in hospitals than three decades ago, far more is being done by auxiliary staff (nonphysicians), and working hours have shortened. A large number of hospital beds were added during the life of the Hill-Burton federal hospital construction program 1948 to 1974, to a point where the number of surplus beds was estimated at 130,000 in 1979.

Medical gadgetry has enormously expanded, with every hospital board eager to have all of the latest contraptions—and using them as fully as possible. The spectacular rise in the number of malpractice suits—and in amounts awarded and the resulting cost of insurance coverage—made duplication or quadruplication of examinations and tests a matter of self-preservation. A congressional committee estimated that unnecessary surgery was rampant and that two million such unnecessary procedures cost over $4 billion in 1977.

Presidential and congressional attempts at cost controls or voluntary restraint failed. Administrative controls are ineffective and cannot overcome the impact of perverse financial incentives which seem to make it desirable for all parties concerned to let costs skyrocket.

A strong national drive toward universal medical insurance coverage has been nearly successful and resulted in almost insulating the patient from the cost of the services he demands and receives. Thus the sky is the limit. Nor can we expect hospitals or physicians to keep their advice and offerings to a minimum as long as we use a reimbursement for service method of payment.

Financial incentives for keeping costs low can be established by prepaid service—which discourages providers from going beyond essential services and by coinsurance which reminds the patient that medical services do not come for free.

A $60 annual medical deductible, as under Medicare B, causes patients to reach the point quickly from which they can buy unlimited amounts of medical dollars for 20 cents each. Small wonder that the federal government now must subsidize Medicare with $10 billion a year, though it was intended to be financed from social insurance contributions.

Medicaid, now utilized by about 10% of the American people, uses no coinsurance nor fee but the most expensive approach, "first dollar" coverage. Is it any surprise that families earning less than $5,000 a year averaged 5.8 physician visits a year in 1977, compared with 4.8 visits by families with an income of $25,000 or over? Is it any wonder that low-income persons receive three times as many days of hospital care as high-income persons?

Congress set a poor example when it reduced the percentage of adjusted gross income which medical expenses must exceed to be income tax deductible from 5% to 3%. There is no reason why a level of normal, recurring and foreseeable medical bills—which total more than the 3% of the tax code or the $60 of Medicare B—should not be borne by the individual directly rather than by higher general tax rates.

The decades old movement for comprehensive national health insurance has seen its best days though its proponents will probably never quit trying to sell that brand of snake oil. Proposals for major medical insurance—often called catastrophic medical insurance—have much to recommend for employee as well as for individual coverage and as a replacement for Medicare. They have strong bipartisan support in Congress and stand a good chance of being phased in over a number of years.

"Major medical" is probably the best and most cost-efficient form of medical insurance. It imposes an adequate deductible amounting to about a normal average of the medical costs which a family or individual should expect to pay just like other living expenses such as food, housing or transportation. It should, however, include a coinsurance clause beyond the deductible, as a (possibly declining) percentage of the total costs, lest it be subjected to abuse.

Of course, no one can really insure his health. All anybody can do is buy insurance to protect himself against the cost of medical care which exceeds what can normally be expected. But we should not forget, as my colleague Rita Ricardo-Campbell has pointed out, that "80% of all medical intervention does not alter the course of disease" and that "the highest life expectancies are found among people who exercise, eat sparingly, and consume far less medical care than the average American."

Housing and Urban Decay

It has been said that the U.S. Department of Housing and Urban Development (HUD), despite its intentions and efforts, is actually presiding over housing and urban decay. That may be an exaggeration. While some of our cities are in a multifaceted decline and appear unable to halt or reverse the downtrend, the condition of American housing is, on the whole, improving, vociferous complaints and sporadic sensational newspaper stories to the contrary notwithstanding.

The Census Bureau found that "substandard" dwelling units dropped from 37% of the housing inventory in 1950 to 9% in 1970 (latest year); subsequent housing surveys reported that deficiencies and inadequacies continued to diminish during the 1970s. Nor is overcrowding an American characteristic. HUD's definition of over-crowding is more than one person per room, while some European countries regard two persons per room to be "normal." The 1976 housing survey found that the number of dwelling units with more than 1.5 persons per room had dropped to 1.0%—from 6.2% in 1950.

We have, over the past three decades, changed from the 2-bedroom to the 3-bedroom home, pushed space of an average single family house from 1100 to 1600 square feet, and filled it with an abundance of the latest technological gadgets. We did it all by enormously expanding credit, repaying our debts years later with cheaper dollars, rejoicing in the multiplication of the value of our home equity. We have, through generous government subsidies, enlarged the ability to consume more housing by persons who contribute little to society or the economy. Someone, of course, has to pay for all this, partially in taxes, direct or indirect, partially in ways that keep him from knowing that he is footing the bill. To a large extent, it is the saver who is getting the short end of the stick; he earns 5% to 8% interest on money that is losing 10% to 13% of its value every year. That is why the United States records the lowest rate of savings (as a percentage of disposable personal income) among industrial countries. That also is

42

why our capital formation and investment in industrial efficiency and expansion are comparatively low. It further is why our rates of productivity growth run low—and have lately turned negative—and economic growth rates are poor.

Despite our huge investment in housing we still have large slums which defy governmental efforts at bulldozing them out of existence. Like the bird Phoenix, they seem to recreate themselves. They are mentioned more often and are more visible than their overseas counterparts because they are spawned in city centers and spread to adjoining areas. In foreign cities, central locations are the preferred choices of prosperous residents who maintain their houses in good repair while slums are kept at a distance and build up on the periphery. Our upper and middle classes have been abandoning downtown sections, and central cities generally, to an impoverished underclass, in a mass flight which has been going on for decades and seems to be accelerating. They mean to escape from abysmal conditions and from repugnant policies of city governments which they found unable to influence, hoping that in surrounding jurisdictions they will achieve at least a semblance of local self-government. Urban policies, largely misguided or mandated from Washington, have proven counterproductive and are largely responsible for progressive deterioration which by now could be irreversible.

The most frequent complaint against urban housing is that it is hard to find and costs too much. Vacancy rates of rental housing in metropolitan areas are running at or below 2% which indicates a shortage. Not much rental housing is being built, very little by private builders, with most of the new construction (70% in 1979) government sponsored or subsidized.

According to official data, the cost of housing has risen only imperceptibly faster than the general price level. Between 1953 (the earliest year for which detailed data are available) and 1978, the Consumer Price Index (CPI) increased by 144%, its housing component by 151%. But there is a wide spread between renting and homeownership: residential rents increased by 104%, homeownership costs by 203%. This means that residential rents, in *constant* dollars, now average one-sixth *less* than they did twenty-five years ago.

That helps to explain the scarcity of rental vacancies. Rents are just too cheap to make leasing an economically worthwhile operation. Some cities maintain rent control at artificially low rents. That causes

43

owners to abandon many thousands of apartment buildings each year because they do not pay their way and become dilapidated. Many other city governments pressure landlords into keeping rents below the market level, with the implicit or explicit threat of imposing rent control if the owners do not comply. To build rental housing has become a losing proposition despite small tax incentives. Most investors and developers will not risk their money on long-range ventures which are not likely to be profitable and may turn sour if rent control is imposed. Nor are many investors keen on becoming the targets of the vilification to which "absentee landlords" are frequently subjected. Renters, on the other hand, hold on to underpriced apartments and consume more space and amenities than they could afford in an open market. It is an inexorable law of economics that goods which by government dictum are priced below open market levels become scarce because of underproduction and overconsumption.

What is in short supply actually is not housing but money—among persons who mean to live at higher standards than their means allow, to consume more of other people's product than they are willing or able to produce in return.

The cost of owner-occupied homes has disproportionately risen. Some of the causes are obvious: the price of land, a scarce commodity of limited supply, has soared from one-eighth of the total cost of the dwelling to one-fourth; wages and materials in construction increased faster than other prices; mortgage interest rates went sky high to keep ahead—ever so slightly—of inflation rates.

But buyers really were not overcharged as home prices multiplied. Most homeowners profited more spectacularly than almost anyone else in recent decades. Suppose a family in 1965 bought a home for $20,000, with a $17,000 mortgage. It downpaid the difference, thus had an equity of $3,000. With the house now worth $60,000 or more, its equity is now worth at least $43,000 (not counting whatever the owner may have paid off on principal). That truly is a spectacular gain on a $3,000 investment.

Small wonder that just about everybody wants to buy a home—or several homes if he can—and puts pressure on government to make credit available on easier terms.

In many ways government has made money available for home purchases more widely and more cheaply than the market and prudent lenders would have done. What counts to most buyers is not

44

so much the price of the house but the size of their monthly payments. With government help they are bidding against each other, which in turn enables sellers to jack up prices. What is driving up construction-related wages and materials prices, land values and the price of homes are governmental programs aiming to expand the range of home buyers (and incidentally help the housing industry) by inflating credit and the money supply. Can this go on forever?

There is no end to this spiral until credit and money supply are restricted to noninflationary levels and a free market is permitted to establish a balance between supply and demand. That could bring an end to the bonanza of people buying houses with government and "other people's" money and paying back loans with dollars that are worth a fraction of what they were, thereby expropriating the savers.

To let home equities soar by supplying large amounts of cheap money to the housing market may fill some owners with joy. But it hardly serves or promotes true equity nor builds a solid base for a prosperous economic future.

Government housing programs are extremely popular and politically virtually unbeatable. What could be more appealing than helping a low-income family get a better place to live, or a young couple, just starting out in life, their first home? Only Scrooge himself could oppose that. The programs are bread and butter to the construction industry—developers, contractors, labor unions—and to lending institutions, providing much of their business. Potential and would-be buyers are of course enthusiastically pushing for more and larger public programs. Nor are current homeowners opposed, knowing that pouring more federal money into home purchases will help the value of their own equities go up faster. The detrimental consequences of such misallocation of huge resources is less visible though the resulting continued underinvestment in *productive* facilities exacts a heavy toll in slower economic growth.

Government housing aid programs take many forms, from rental assistance to subsidies to local public housing authorities; from homeownership assistance to tax exempt bonds financing low-interest mortgages and more than a dozen others. Their costs are nowhere totaled. HUD outlays for housing programs in FY 1980 are estimated at $6 billion but budgetary authority, that is, commitment for payments extending for 20 to 40 years at $29 billion. Accumulated HUD obligations for future payments amounted to $250 billion at the end of FY 1980 and are estimated to total $278 billion at the end of FY 1981. That type of federal debt is now rising at close to $30 billion a year but is not included in the national debt nor in the budget outlays.

Housing assistance is intended to aid low-income families. But definitions of low income have been inching up. Subsidies enable a family just below the income ceiling to pay less for better quarters than a family barely above the line has to lay out for poorer accommodations—from its own earnings. This inequity has fueled a drive to push up income ceilings to middle-income levels, leading to hot congressional debates on just where to draw the line.

A higher income ceiling for subsidy eligibility can multiply political support for a program, but also its cost to the taxpayer. HUD generally subsidizes rentals which exceed 15% to 25% of a family's income. This enables many households to occupy more spacious, modern, more generously equipped apartments in better locations than they could afford from their own means.

At 1980 congressional hearings the secretary of HUD testified that because of inadequate appropriations only one-fifth of the families which under departmental definitions are eligible for subsidies are actually being helped. This opens vistas of a huge potential expansion whenever Congress is willing to multiply appropriations.

The Nixon administration, in its early years, attempted to develop less expensive methods of construction, especially for low-income housing. Operation *Breakthrough* was launched with the expectation that it would live up to its name. It soon ran into fierce opposition from the construction industries—labor and management—which disliked the idea of replacing local builders and labor with industrial methods, and from organizations on the political left which were appalled by the proposition to supply "disadvantaged" people with "cheap" housing. Under fire from both sides, operation *Breakthrough* fizzled out after a few years.

To many others, the idea of using factory-produced housing instead of old-fashioned craft methods seemed appealing and led to wider use of so-called mobile homes. They are not truly mobile and rarely move. But manufactured housing can be turned out through assembly-line methods at one-third the cost of traditional houses. Thereby it offers the only way in which many elderly couples of limited means can afford to buy their own home; most of the owners treasure them as their most valuable asset and maintain them well. But mobile homes never managed to gain favor with low-income, welfare or other publicly assisted families and turned out to be not strong enough to withstand for any length of time the treatment they would be accorded by those tenants. Less expensive types of construction thus turned out to be unsuitable for housing tenants at the lowest income levels. With no stake in their dwelling, they proved adept at converting even traditionally built houses, and entire sections, into instant slums.

The inordinate spread of structural decay in city cores became a source of public concern after World War II and motivated Congress to authorize in 1949 a vast *Urban Renewal Program*. Initiated with great hopes and enthusiasm, the program's results disillusioned its supporters within a few years. By the time it was left to expire in 1974, it was utterly discredited.

During its 25-year life, Urban Renewal led to the construction of some magnificent downtown office and shopping centers on cleared slum sites but, in the process, destroyed about three times as many dwellings as it built. Most of the small number of new apartments were beyond the economic reach of the people who had formerly lived there. The families moved to adjoining sections of town which they soon turned into slums just like those that had been bulldozed out of existence.

Urban Renewal and related programs were undertaken on faith, not on research, and based on the naive assumption that bad housing is at the core of urban deterioration and the cause of social ills such as family breakup, welfare dependency, delinquency, vagrancy, vandalism, street crime and other offenses. It was then widely believed that people's and a city's social conditions could be uplifted by wiping out slums and liberalizing welfare programs. It did not turn out that way. It is far harder to change people, to the extent to which this can be done, than to erect gleaming new structures. Slums can move to other locations but they cannot, in today's American cities, be eliminated as experience in the 1950s and 1960s proved. *Slums are not decaying buildings; slums are people.*

Major efforts were undertaken to replace rundown housing with new and clean structures through public housing and publicly subsidized housing. Because land costs devour a disproportionate share of the outlay in single homes, attention shifted to multistory construction which in foreign cities accounts for most low-income housing, and, in fact, for much of all urban housing. But in the United States highrises for poverty people turned into disasters.

Eleven-storied Pruitt-Igoe, built in St. Louis in 1954 as a showpiece of what public housing can be at its best, soon demonstrated what it can be at its worst. Neglect, abuse, vandalism, crime and tenant warfare against the management turned the project into a nightmare. In 1972 several of its 23 buildings had to be dynamited because their occupants had made them uninhabitable beyond a possibility of restoration. Pruitt-Igoe was the most infamous case of its kind, but unfortunately not the only one.

Highrises are no longer being constructed for public housing. Low-income housing is being built battle-proof to give it a chance of surviving under combat conditions. The cost of repairs and cleaning have many or most public housing authorities tottering on the brink of bankruptcy from which they are periodically rescued by Uncle Sam. No one has yet found an alternative to the large subsidies the projects require to remain suitable for human occupancy. Private landlords in deteriorating urban sections have for decades been abandoning their property by the tens of thousands, unable to sustain big losses for an indefinite period.

When Urban Renewal ended in the mid-1970s, it was replaced by a congeries of programs for "community development" which poured even larger annual amounts into similar purposes with positive results yet to be determined.

There has been much talk about "revitalizing" the cities. But no one has yet been able to come up with a miracle cure. No plan of that type offers much hope for success unless it can reverse the mass flight from cities.

It is not a "white flight" as is sometimes claimed. Black upper and middle classes are moving out too, while poor whites stay. It is a flight of families which can *afford* to move. Many more would do likewise— if they could.

It is a flight from all-pervasive crime which cannot be cured by hiring a few more policemen as long as criminals are receiving kid-glove treatment from courts and politicians. It is a flight from schools whose educational quality is going down for lack of standards of learning and discipline that cannot be corrected by building a few "magnet" schools nor by any amount of forced busing. It is a flight from federal policies which are destroying the cities' economic and demographic support bases. The policies were, of course, not so intended; but they could not be much different if they were.

It is not just that cities are losing numbers, but they are losing the people they need most and attracting the people of whom they already have too many. Productive people are moving out and dependent people are moving in. The latter are being made more comfortable by generous public programs; the former driven out by high taxes and perverse policies.

With half or more of some cities' population dependent on city government for employment or support, it is questionable whether officials can still be elected who promise to reverse the trend of more soft jobs and higher welfare benefits. Cities are losing job opportunities by the hundreds of thousands because many industrial and commercial firms which are not compelled to locate in city centers by the nature of their business, prefer to move to jurisdictions where they are less likely to be harassed and become objects of exploitation and where they and their employees can feel and are safer. Could "free enterprise zones" which have recently been suggested turn the downward trend around? It might have to be tried. But without many other policy changes they probably could not pull enough weight.

Urban plight is often viewed as a problem of insufficient city revenues which can be resolved by the infusion of larger federal funds. That's been tried, with questionable results. Among governments as well as among individuals, lack of sufficient money usually is not the *cause* of a problem but its *manifestation* and *consequence*. By treating the symptom we may be able to make the patient feel less uncomfortable but we cannot thereby cure him. In alleviating his aches and fever, we may also weaken his sense of urgency, the intensity of his efforts to get at the root of the trouble. We may thus enable him to live with it for a long time by feeding him even larger doses of a painkiller until, mercifully, life itself ebbs.

Mayors have long been seeking relief and redemption by clamoring for ever larger amounts of federal aid. Money, in whatever form and for whatever purpose, can make life easier and more pleasant for city officials, help them avoid the tough decisions that otherwise they would have to make. It can enhance incumbents' popularity among city employees and beneficiaries of services and funds and their own re-electability. It can postpone, time and again, the day of reckoning and may be able to defer it until the term of that mayor's successor's successor. But it cannot restore the city's basic health nor the human, economic, social foundation a city needs to live on and prosper.

Can cities again be made places so desirable to live in that *productive* people, people who can help support the city rather than be supported by it, will *want* to move back? No one can tell but some of the actions required will politically not be easy to adopt and carry out. Some of the major actions are within the realm of the national government, its legislative, executive and judicial branches, and beyond the authority of city, and even state governments. But city and state officials will have to play a major role in such a program if it is to have a chance of success.

To make cities again safe places to live, calls for steps which are beyond the powers of the police chief, the police commissioner, the mayor, though they'll have to do their share. They must make it sufficiently unpleasant for criminals to pursue their preferred activities within city jurisdiction. Federal and state legislatures, courts, chief executives hold the master keys to action that could reduce incidence of crime to tolerable levels. Without drastic measures at the federal level, local officials lack the authority to do what needs to be done.

Nor is an uplift of public school education within the province of city councils. Boards of education which once ruled school systems have become mere pawns in the hands of federal courts and federal bureaucrats. Again, it is Congress and state legislatures which must lay down the ground rules for returning authority to elected or appointed local officials. Unless educational standards and discipline can be raised and schools can again pursue excellence rather than uniform mediocrity and the children's safety can be assured, few parents will return.

The power which public labor unions wield over their own governments, to have the largest number of well-paid—and often overpaid—employees must be broken.

Federal and state governments have turned city governments into huge social welfare operations and city officials have cooperated in return for greater financial support. This has made cities more attractive to dependent persons and unattractive to the people the cities need. Social welfare for its needy residents must continue to be a major task of urban government. But it must be scaled to more reasonable and tolerable levels than exist at present.

The energy shortage which will continue for a long time may offer an opportunity as well as a challenge. Cities continue to hold a majority of jobs in the private economy and the cost of commuting to the city center has become a sizable burden on workers who fled to distant suburbs. This may cause some to consider moving closer to their place of work if conditions in such locations are made tolerable. Meanwhile, commuter driving over long distances is becoming too expensive and an inexcusable waste of scarce fuel.

Mass transportation must increasingly replace individual driving. Rapid rail transit systems are not a feasible answer in any but a few of the largest cities, and new construction is too exorbitant to consider. Government transit subsidies to finance huge current deficits must be sharply curtailed by drastic operating economies—especially of excessive wage rates—and by raising fares substantially. Wider use of buses, minibuses, jitneys, carpools, company vans are the most likely alternatives to rail transit or personal automobiles. How can individual drivers be taken out of their cars and forced into mass transportation?

Mass transportation is inconvenient to persons who have been used to driving to and from work and every other place they want to go. Chauffeuring is ego satisfying and Americans have developed a love affair with their own car. They will yield only to irresistible economic pressure. They will drastically reduce individual driving if either it is made prohibitively expensive—by catching drivers "on the run or on the roost"—or if it is made impossible by gasoline rationing.

The federal government's policy of forbidding tolls on highways it subsidized was counterproductive to begin with and should now be repealed. If the use of private cars on city streets and expressways were gradually reduced, traffic could speed up and buses could then provide faster transportation than individual commuting ever did. Rush hour traffic jams could become a thing of the past.

No mass movement *to* the cities can be expected even under the best of circumstances. But if the mass flight *from* the cities can be halted, and slowly be reversed, the prospects for the future of at least some of the cities could look much brighter than they do now. No one should put his hopes too high for some of our older cities, especially those in the "frost belt" which have been on the downgrade for a long time. With a diminishing economic and demographic base, and with a growing imbalance in voting patterns with regard to public policies, some of our cities may be beyond the point of no return. The alternatives I outlined may be difficult to put into practice. But there may be no other alternative to an eventual ruin of many of America's cities.

Civil Rights and Civil Wrongs:
Color-blind or Race-conscious Policies?

At the core of most of the social programs I discussed in the preceding pages, their explosive growth and exorbitant cost, lies the minorities problem. Minorities participate disproportionately in public welfare programs because many of them do not succeed as well as others in climbing the rungs of the economic ladder. That is why so many continually depend on governmental assistance.

Their disadvantage tends to start early in life. Coming from poor homes, they average one to several years behind grade level in the three Rs and other basic knowledge, although public schools devote no smaller, and often greater, resources and efforts to the education of minority children. Though those students now attend school for about as many years as anybody else, many of them do not acquire comparable vocational skills and subsequently do not rise as high in the occupational ranks. Relatively few advance to eminent positions, to prosperity or wealth. Many remain in low-level, ill-paid, dead-end jobs and a high percentage of them wind up in an underclass, condemned to a lifelong struggle for an austere and often dismal existence. Far too many turn into social problems.

It is always easier to name a problem than to agree on its nature, causes and possible cures. We may start by trying to define what we mean by minorities. As the home of a nation composed of immigrants from many lands and descents, America is inhabited by nothing but ethnic minorities. But when we talk about minorities nowadays, we usually refer to people who in the aggregate equal close to one-fifth of the U.S. population, with about 90% of them belonging to two groups:

    1. Blacks, mostly descendants of slaves brought from Africa in the 1700s and the early 1800s, who account for about three-fifths of the total;

    2. Hispanics, that is, individuals most of whose ancestors prior to the mass arrival of European settlers lived in the southern part of what later became United States territory or who subsequently immigrated from south of the border.

The remainder of the American people, with the exception of a few smaller groups such as American Indians, Eskimos, Filipinos, etc. accounting for less than 10% of the minorities, are called nonminorities, or simply, the "majority."

It may thus appear that minorities can be defined as nonwhite people, as persons of non-European descent. Many so believe, but it is an oversimplification which confuses the issues and does not help to ease or solve the problems. What causes the societal problems is not color of skin but statistically identifiable socioeconomic characteristics. Members of minorities are two to four times as likely to be poor, unemployed, welfare-dependent, functionally illiterate, to belong to a female-headed household, be arrested or in prison.

But the crucial fact is that the majority of the poor, unemployed, welfare-dependent, illiterate, criminal offenders, prisoners, and member of the "underclass" if you please, are white. Furthermore, that the majority of what we call minorities is not unemployed, poor, welfare-dependent, illiterate or in prison. Most members of the "minorities" hold a job, support themselves and their families, can read and write, and do not run afoul of our criminal laws.

The line that separates the problem population from the rest of our people is *not* the color line. It is economic, social and various other characteristics and personal traits. The true minorities are not people with nonwhite faces, but persons who, for whatever reason, remain far below the attainments and standards of our affluent society. We cannot eliminate the lowest ten percent or twenty percent on a statistical distribution of income, achievement in education, business, art, athletics, or any other field, nor in strength, health, beauty, or any other endowment. No matter what we do, there will always remain a bottom ten percent who will cry, "Why me?"

If we draw the division along color lines, we focus on factors which are unchangeable, essentially irrelevant, and by themselves do not cause the critical problems. By drawing the line along socioeconomic and related characteristics, we aim at identifying the core of the problem which, possibly, we can do something about.

By ethnic classification, persons of Chinese and Japanese descent are minorities. By socioeconomic characteristics, they are hardly distinguishable from the majority. The Cubans who settled in the Miami area in the 1960s and 1970s built a prosperous community with none of the disadvantages that beset so many of the Mexican immigrants. This was not because Cubans and Mexicans belong to different ethnic groups, but because many of the Cubans were educated, middle-class, professional or business people who had fled the Castro regime for political reasons. Most of the Mexicans came from an impoverished peasant background, had left their native villages because they could not earn an adequate living there and found it difficult in their new surroundings to adjust quickly to unaccustomed demands and conditions. The difference between Cubans and Mexicans was cultural, not racial.

Some federal programs recognize the socioeconomic rather than ethnic nature of minority status. Allocations to schools under the compensatory education program (Title I of the Elementary and Secondary Education Act of 1965) are based on parental income, not on ethnic classification. Many other government actions, however, focus on ethnic labels.

There is a statistical overlap between socioeconomic and ethnic data. The "gap" between ethnic minorities and national totals has been narrowing but remains wide. Members of designated ethnic minorities have, on the average, not attained educational, occupational, economic or social equality with other Americans. The reasons may be manyfold, are highly contended and opinions polarized. Among the less controversial explanations are certain historical facts.

For nearly a century after emancipation, most blacks continued to live an extremely poor rural existence. Few were prepared for life in a competitive city environment, for a job hustle into which mass migration to the North from about the 1940s on threw them. To bridge a gap of generations or centuries is a difficult task which can be speeded up only to a limited extent. No hopes raised by empty promises of ambitious politicians, no impatience generated thereby, can telescope it any more than it can shorten a gestation period. The abyss between 17th century African bush and 19th century share-cropper life on one hand and the demands of a contemporary high-pressure urban society on the other can be jumped only by a small number of highly gifted individuals. For most others, it takes more time, usually generations.

Most Hispanics also came from a bare subsistence and extremely primitive peasant life that did not prepare them for what they would face in cities founded centuries earlier by European settlers who had many centuries of cultural tradition behind them. To put the Hispanics' poverty status in the United States in the right perspective we should not forget how much poorer they were in their former habitats south of the border.

Racial discrimination unquestionably slowed the progress of minorities. But to attribute remaining discrepancies between minorities and majority entirely or mostly to continuing prejudice and bias is too simple, and too glib an explanation, and simply not adequate. The ethnic minorities which came here in earlier times, the Italians, Poles, Greeks, Irish, Scandinavians, Germans and even most Dutch and Anglo-Saxons, were not met at Ellis Island by welcoming committees with open arms. They were subjected to deliberate, sustained and open discrimination and exploitation. That was their tuition fee or admission ticket. Jews, Chinese, Japanese could tell stories of undisguised and vicious racism and outright persecution. Most of the immigrants and their children lived a wretched existence and were destitute for long periods. That does not seem to have left "indelible scars" on the newcomers nor on their offspring.

None of the hundreds of assistance programs which are now available existed, nor public welfare; no or very few poor schools were accessible to the newcomers' children. But they toiled and sweated for small pay with most of them working their way up gradually to a middle-class or better status, without government aid. Some of the immigrants did not quite "make it." They turned into an underclass which in more recent decades was joined by other newcomers to the technological age, who found coping with sophisticated competitive surroundings difficult and, in every sense of the word, were minorities.

Racial bias and prejudice have not been entirely wiped out but, in contrast to earlier times, are no longer practiced openly, and certainly far less widely. To hurry up adjustments, government tried, from about the 1940s on, to equalize opportunities for all and to proscribe racial discrimination. Civil rights legislation in the 1960s added statutory sanctions to recognized and broadly accepted moral principles. All decisions by government and private parties on education, employment, housing, etc. are, by law, now to be made "without regard to race, creed, color or national origin." This has helped to narrow the statistical "gap" between minorities and majority.

Given the wide range of human traits and faculties, a policy of offering *equal opportunity* to all, is bound to produce results which differ as widely as do capacities and aspirations among individuals.

55

Substantial statistical differences remained between various ethnic groups with regard to learning achievements—as shown by tests, grades, examinations, admissions, graduation—in employment—with regard to hiring or joblessness, promotions, advancement to management positions—in income and other socioeconomic yardsticks, in athletics, arts and in most other fields of human endeavor.

That appalled civil rights advocates who had believed that equal opportunity would produce equal results. When it did not, they shifted from the principle of equal opportunity to a goal of equal results. Equal results, however, given a wide range of capacities, can be brought about only by unequal opportunities. Thus in the 1960s, statutes and rules which mandated that decisions had to be made "without regard to race, etc." were interpreted as authorizing and demanding that race, color, etc. become a prime consideration of actions in education and employment.

It is a supreme irony that civil rights legislation which in impeccable language mandated equal treatment "without regard to race, color, etc." could be so perverted as to allow and impose racial preferences.

To be sure, federal agencies did not order employers to give preference to members of certain ethnic groups over others. But they demanded, under sanction of law, that employers establish numerical hiring goals for ethnic groups which could be achieved in no way except by preferential treatment. *Affirmative Action*—a euphemism for reverse discrimination—is by its own definition "goal oriented." That means that goals must be reached without regard to methods, and that the end justifies the means. A "color-blind" policy, which by definition provides equal opportunity among ethnic groups, is now anathema. Its advocates are denounced as racists. Language has been so perverted that an "equal opportunity employer" now is an employer who agrees to grant preference to ethnic minorities. The *Equal Employment Opportunity Commission*, created in 1964 to resolve charges of racial and other discrimination, with the help of nearly 4,000 employees, now forces employers to discriminate against individuals who do not belong to designated ethnic groups—although the Civil Rights Act of 1964 specifies that no employer could be required "to grant preferential treatment to any individual or group because of race, color, religion, sex or national origin." Numerical goals compel companies to recruit, hire, promote persons with a Spanish surname over applicants with French, German, Italian or Polish surnames.

Does this not violate the equal rights clause of the Fourteenth Amendment?

The U.S. Supreme Court found in 1978:

> It is clear beyond cavil that the obligation imposed by Title VII [of the Civil Rights Act] is to provide an equal opportunity for each applicant regardless of race, without regard to whether members of the applicant's race are already proportionately represented in the work force.

In 1971 the Court declared:

> Discriminatory preference for any group, minority or majority, is precisely and only what Congress has proscribed. . . . Congress has made such [job-related] qualifications the controlling factor, so that race, religion, nationality, and sex become irrelevant.

But irrelevant is exactly what race did *not* become. In several cases such as Bakke, Weber, Fullilove, the Court has upheld racial quotas or race as a valid consideration in employment and admission decisions. Racial quotas, labeled "numerical goals" are now being forced on employers all over the country because their employees do not, by numbers or rank, reflect general population ratios of some ethnic groups. Even the federal government, after four decades of nondiscrimination rules and a shorter period of affirmative action efforts, has not been able to achieve proportionate representation. The Armed Services in which in 1980 21.6% of the enlisted personnel was black but only 4.8% of the officers, are rather typical of the record in most federal departments under civil service, including the Department of Justice, and in the federal courts.

In the waning days of the Carter administration, the Department of Justice undertook to phase out the Professional and Administrative Career Examination (PACE), the most important civil service test for 118 federal middle- and upper-level positions. When a large number of black and Hispanic applicants failed the tests, the government prepared to set up new tests and to guarantee that a certain proportion of minority candidates would pass the tests and get jobs. Parallel action had been taken in the lower civil service grades from about 1970 on. This easing of the threshold not only lowered the qualifications of new accessions but depressed morale and effectiveness generally as it was viewed as an abandonment of the competitive merit principle based on objective criteria which had been the cornerstone of the civil service for nearly a century. Affirmative Action is forcing private business enterprises to observe the same principles—with similar impact on productivity.

The State Department which has always looked upon the Foreign Service as its elite corps—and accepts only between 2 and 3 of every 100 applicants, who must pass a tough written exam—allows minority candidates to skip the exam or pass it at a lower score than whites. That only illustrates what is increasingly becoming routine throughout the federal establishment, in the armed services and, under growing pressure from federal civil rights offices and courts, in private employment, as well as in admission to universities, colleges and graduate schools.

In his dissent with the Supreme Court's "separate but equal" decision in 1896 Justice Harlan wrote:

> Our constitution is color-blind, and neither knows nor tolerates classes among citizens. In respect to civil rights, all citizens are equal before the law.

The U.S. Constitution, federal civil rights laws and regulations issued thereunder ordain in clear and unequivocal terms *a color-blind* policy of equal rights and treatment for all. Enforcement by federal agencies, however, does not allow employers, educational institutions and others to hire, promote, admit, graduate individuals *without* regard to race, color, etc. They insist on *color-conscious* policies. The U.S. Supreme Court, usually with the narrowest majorities and in a low and uncertain voice, has acquiesced. Thus we now have in the United States two sets of law—as some southern states did for many years: one for designated ethnic minorities, one for everybody else.

In no field has a color-conscious policy wrought worse damage than in education. The Supreme Court's intent in outlawing state-imposed school segregation was clearly spelled out in *Brown II* (1955): ". . . to achieve a system of determining admission to the public schools on a nonracial basis . . . ." This was a long overdue step which Congress and the state legislatures ought to have taken far earlier. They, rather than the Court, would have been the appropriate authority to establish the new rule which was in the nature of an amendment more than an interpretation of the constitution.

Maybe the Court which in 1896 had pronounced the "separate but equal" doctrine, felt that it should overrule itself—more precisely, the incumbent justices' predecessors—in keeping with the country's conscience at mid-century. Who could have guessed at that time that subsequent decisions of the Supreme Court would extend a policy of determining admission to the public schools on a *racial* basis—which prior to 1954 existed only in a few southern states—to cover school districts all over the United States?

Previously, black children would be refused admission to white schools and white children to black schools. Now, black children are refused admission to black schools, white children to white schools. Does that spell "equal justice under the law?"

How was such a 180 degree turn possible, how could the Court within less than two decades begin to compel school authorities to assign children on a racial basis—which the Court had found repugnant—and do it against strong and widespread objections and resistance? It is an almost unbelievable story—and it probably could not happen anywhere else in the world. But it did happen in the 1970s, by judicial mandate, with no legislative approval, and in the face of overwhelming coast-to-coast popular opposition—in a country that prides itself on its "government by the people."

Congress did order school desegregation and defined it in the *Civil Rights Act of 1964* as follows:

> "Desegregation" means the assignment of students to public schools and within such schools without regard to their race, color, religion or national origin, but "desegregation" shall not mean the assignment of students to public schools in order to overcome racial imbalance.

When courts began to issue busing orders in the early 1970s, Congress decreed in the *Equal Educational Opportunities Act of 1974*:

> No court, department or agency of the United States shall . . . order the implementation of a plan that would require the transportation of any student to a school other than the school closest or next closest to his place of residence which provides the appropriate grade level and type of education for such student.

The Supreme Court bypassed congressional restrictions on busing to overcome racial imbalance by designating as its objective "to eliminate

59

from the public schools all vestiges of state-imposed segregation." But courts subsequently issued busing orders for cities from Boston to Los Angeles, which had never known state-imposed segregation.

A goal "to eliminate . . . all vestiges of state-imposed segregation" could have been accomplished in southern states by giving students the right freely to choose the school they wished to attend. When some of those states adopted "freedom of choice" plans, not many children shifted to other schools—up to 15–20% of black children, very few of the white. So, in 1968 the Supreme Court turned racial mixing from a civil right to a civil duty and in 1971 began to approve compulsory busing orders. Judges tried to justify such orders by claiming that city councils or school boards had, by indirect action, contributed to predominantly minority attendance at some schools, predominantly white attendance at others.

What motivated the Supreme Court to commit the "bus blunder" and thereby *de facto* overrule its commitment to nonracial assignment? We can only speculate. A major concern of all authorities was the low achievements, the educational "lag" of black children. Only about 15% of them perform at a level which 50% of the white children attain. For a long time low scores on national standard tests were attributed to the schools' inadequate financial support. But studies beginning with the largest school survey ever, *Equality of Educational Opportunity*, directed by James Coleman of Johns Hopkins University in 1965 found to their surprise that there was no difference in terms of resource input—per student expenditures, teacher-student ratios, teacher qualifications, teacher salaries, physical facilities, etc.— between schools attended by black and white children. Backup studies confirmed those findings. Nor was there evidence that magnitude of the schools' income affected the educational outcome.

Differences in performance are wider *within* schools and classes than *among* schools. This suggests that what the children bring to school accounts for more than what they find at school. Attempts to raise basic skills and knowledge among lagging children through smaller classes, compensatory education, community control of schools (black or Hispanic), performance contracting and dozens of other reforms and experiments, costing many billions, were no more successful in "closing the gap" in measurable skills.

The alibi of insufficient funds wore threadbare as per student expenditures soared and low scores on national standard tests became

60

a source of embarrassment to many schools. That led to a campaign to abolish standard tests altogether and thereby prevent evidence of the gap from being produced.

When that campaign made only slow progress—faced by public demand for more rather than less information on educational quality—there seemed to be only one avenue left, and the Supreme Court pointed at it in a 1971 decision: make it impossible to identify a school as white or black. Since families cannot be ordered to move en masse to other neighborhoods, busing of students seemed to be the only method of bringing about a uniform racial mix, a "balance," in each school.

Busing did not raise the educational performance of black children. It forced schools which had been trying to maintain relatively high standards of curriculum, grading, promotion to compromise when they were faced with the influx of large numbers of bused-in children who were not able to meet those standards. Teachers and administrators had little choice but to shift to levels which the new students could grasp and assimilate. The "gap" between the aggregate test scores of many formerly predominantly black schools and white schools tended to narrow. Schools might have moved toward a situation where average test scores would not have differed too widely among them, if integration through busing had succeeded. It failed when a growing number of parents began to "vote with their feet" when they felt that their children's learning and safety were threatened and that escape was the only possible solution. Families either moved out of the district's jurisdiction or sent their children to private schools. Within a few months—or at most a year or two—schools subjected to forced busing moved from *desegregation* to *resegregation*, from *integration* to *disintegration*. The nation's major urban public school systems became predominantly minority—ethnic as well as socioeconomic.

This has been called a "white flight"—which it was not. Middle- and upper-class parents, white, black, Hispanic, were equally unwilling to send their children to schools whose educational and disciplinary standards they regarded to be unacceptable and which continued to fall, to schools where violence and vandalism reigned.

Aljean Harmetz, a *New York Times* reporter, described events in Los Angeles in the summer of 1980, when only 27% of the students remaining in the city's public school system were white. After stating, "we considered ourselves liberals. We believed in integration," she gradually turned to "a sense of outrage" when she realized "the kind of education available at the end of the bus ride in the school where the reading and math scores were 50 points below our own," and when she became worried about her own daughter's safety. She concluded "that it was only numbers that mattered to the court, that our children were merely statistics in computer simulations." ("School Rage," *New West*, October 20, 1980.)

Outmigration from the cities during the 1970s was about 11% black—approximately the percentage of blacks in the population. This was not a white flight; it was a middle-class flight. The outmigrants—as well as those who remained behind—could more appropriately be identified in socioeconomic terms than by racial labels. The critical fact is not that the public school systems of major cities turned black and Hispanic but that they increasingly enrolled students of low achievements and aspirations. Demands for higher educational quality could not be met by boosting standards because much of the student body would not be able to live up to them.

When court orders on forced busing drove ever larger numbers of middle-class families to the suburbs while central city schools turned increasingly low-class, black, Hispanic, demands arose for metro-politan area-wide busing. Children could then be shuttled between the central city and its suburbs and their escape route cut off, except to private schools, which only a limited number of parents can afford. Several federal district courts issued metro busing orders but the Supreme Court so far has not upheld them. It disapproved of compulsory interdistrict busing. It did so with narrow margins and in less than firm language, thus leaving the door open to a possible later reversal if the scenario were but slightly changed.

If the High Court were to order metro-wide busing, to overcome the failure of intra-district busing to bring about a desired uniform racial mix, it could pave the way to general school integration—if the Court's mandate were carried out. There is, however, a good chance that, just as in *Dred Scott* in 1857, the consequences might be quite different from what the Court expected. Attempts to force an interchange of children between city and suburban schools could generate a national movement strong enough to cause Congress and the state legislatures to act strongly where in the past they have tended to react in a soft and hesitant manner. It could lead to adoption of a constitutional amendment to outlaw race-conscious policies generally. That would restore a government of the people. That government could then begin to tackle the real problems in education, employment and other areas related to minorities.

In Conclusion   The presence of sizable minorities raises intricate problems in many countries. None of them has dealt with the problem in a worse manner than the United States whose government is turning difficulty into disaster. It is the welfare state run amuck which, dominated by egalitarian ideas, set its sights not on equal *opportunity* for all but on equal *results*. It thereby violates the basic rights of persons by treating them not as individuals but as members of a group with rights that supersede those of individuals. While paying lip service to treatment "without regard to race or color," it imposed, in an incredible reversal of the equal rights principle, race-conscious policies, especially in education and employment. This was not done by the people's representatives through legislation. It was not done by elective officials who, being dependent on popular approval, could not have taken and politically survived action contrary to the concepts and moral principles of an overwhelming majority of their constituents. It was done by nonelected officials, most of them appointed for life, who usurped a power that was constitutionally not theirs. They did so in utter noncomprehension of the nature and intricacy of the matters they were undertaking to decide and accomplished it by outrageous perversion of language.

It could not have happened if the action had been subject to veto by the people. Numerous polls have proven that most Americans want and demand nonracial public policies. By majorities of better than three to one respondents to public opinion polls have consistently declared their belief in equal treatment without regard to ethnic origin and their opposition to racial quotas or goals, in schools, places of employment, athletics and other fields.

I stated my beliefs regarding the minorities problem in 1966 as follows:

> It seems to me that there is no solution to the ethnic minority, or race, or color, or Negro problem in the United States until we quit looking at it and treating it as an ethnic or race or color or Negro problem. . . .
>
> The challenge this country faces is not of a racial nature—though

fierce attempts are being made here—as they were and are being made in many foreign lands—to turn it into a race conflict. The challenge is of people who are poor, ignorant, without jobs, who behave badly or criminally toward themselves, their families, their neighbors or others and toward society.

To know that some of them are white, black, red or yellow does not help us; it only confuses the issue and may make a peaceful solution well-nigh unattainable. Opportunity to avoid increasing violence, strife, and maybe chaos and rebellion, is offered by a public policy that is color-blind. It may be our only chance. [*Congressional Record*, September 13, 1966, p. 21547.]

I still so hold.

Well-intentioned but Ill-conceived

In several chapters of this book I discussed major governmental activities and their growth. Many of the programs yielded a meager return to the taxpayers, some turned out to be counterproductive. Most of the expansion was brought about by the efforts of sincere groups which, driven by the best of intentions but limited by tunnel vision, saw the public interest in terms of their own concepts of what society and the universe ought to be, viewed it as being identical with their own interests, and pursued goals consonant with their members' personal stakes. Since special interest groups tend to be more strongly dedicated to their ideas and better organized than associations focusing on the general interest, they prevail more often than mere numbers would lead us to expect.

Besides the major fields which I covered, there are hundreds of other activities regarding which we must ask government: Are you helping to solve the problem or are you part of the problem? Time and again, government has perpetuated a problem that would have solved itself long ago if there had been no interference, because the individuals involved would have seen no alternative but to get their own hands dirty and take care of the matter themselves.

But the principle of individual responsibility is anathema to the runaway welfare state, whose philosophy of excuse and alibi holds all shortcomings and deficiencies to be the fault of society which it is government's duty to remedy, cure or make up for. "Government's duty" in this case means that those who face up to their challenges and resolve problems by their own efforts will also be shouldered with the burden of others who deftly manage to shift it on to them. That is the purpose for which hundreds of governmental programs were created and expanded and for which thousands of regulations were drafted and imposed.

The rejection of personal responsibility for an undesired turn of events, the outward projection of what often is the result of the individual's inadequate concern, planning, precaution, preparation, effort or plain neglect or unwillingness to face unpleasant facts, expresses the spirit of a wayward welfare state. It manifests itself in the multiplication of public programs and, in cases where government cannot be held directly liable, in the growth of litigation, with everybody suing everybody else. Much of the cost of litigation is passed on by insurance, through taxes, through higher prices, to organizations, to public or private legal aid, so that the risk and direct cost of going to court often are low. But of course we all pay the price in the end, no matter who happens to sign the first check.

A contributing factor to the growth of litigation is the increasing frequency of failures, malfunctions, breakdowns, recalls, maintenance problems, of repairs incompetently or carelessly done, of sloppy service, which manifest a widespread breakdown of quality in our society, a failure to uphold and enforce standards. People do not care to toil hard in an egalitarian society which does not recognize nor adequately rewards individual achievement nor penalizes failure. The impact of the welfare state goes far beyond the programs it operates.

Donald Lambro, in a fascinating book *Fat City*, listed "100 Nonessential Federal Programs" and estimated

> that at least $100 billion a year in taxes is unnecessarily going to the federal government to be squandered on programs our country could better do without; wasteful programs that belong at the bottom of any national ranking of social priorities; programs whose original purpose for being no longer exists; programs that serve only a tiny fraction of the people at the expense of the nation as a whole; programs that duplicate what is already being done by the private sector. . . .
>
> Tens of billions of dollars are lost each year by the federal government through fraud, mismanagement, abuse, waste, error, and sheer extravagance.[15]

There can be disagreement regarding some of the activities which Mr. Lambro calls nonessential. But, give or take some, it adds up to a stunning indictment of the use to which much of the American taxpayer's money is put.

The $100 billion total need not be taken literally. The total could be far more—or less. A presidential commission placed the cost of federal paperwork at $100 billion—half borne by private industry. Experts on regulatory activities estimated the cost of government regulation to the public at the same amount. No one knows the real cost of those activities because major aspects can only be guessed and much depends on value judgments. But in today's world, it probably takes a figure with at least a dozen digits to look impressive—and $100,000,000,000 is the lowest amount to fill that requirement.

Government as Regulator

The need for government regulation of some activities is self-evident if the people are to be protected against certain perils against which they cannot otherwise adequately defend themselves. American preference has generally been for letting the market make most economic decisions, wherever there is competition. To preserve an open market, antitrust legislation was passed in the late XIX century and its enforcement gradually strengthened against "conspiracy in restraint of trade" by management, though not by organized labor—whose monopoly status has been favored and aided by official policy for nearly half a century. That deliberate imbalance was at the time intended to offset an imbalance in economic power. Whether that argument still has validity has become questionable. The economic impact of the policy may be counterproductive but it is firmly rooted in the political facts of life, considering relative voting strengths.

Industrial regulation began in fields in which competition was weak or nonexistent—some of them called natural monopolies—such as transportation (railroads, trucking), communications (telephone), energy (electric power and gas). Some industries were regulated to protect consumers (e.g., insurance, banking and finance), others to protect producers (agriculture). Gradually the principle of regulation became popular among some of the affected businesses because, in the words of (then) chairman of the Federal Trade Commission Lewis A. Engman, "much of today's regulatory machinery does little more than shelter producers from the normal competitive consequences of lassitude and inefficiency." Recent drives to deregulate trucking and

66

airlines, which were partially successful, were opposed by management because they interfered with a more comfortable routine. On the whole, however, most businesses feel that they are overregulated, hounded and harassed by regulatory agencies. That is why Congress, being aware of what it was doing, wisely exempted itself from each regulatory law it enacted—from the National Labor Relations Act of 1935 and the Civil Rights Act of 1964 to the Occupational Safety and Health Act of 1970 and the Equal Opportunities Act of 1972. One congressman was reported to say to a colleague: "I'd hate to have to do business under the laws we just passed." Strangely enough, the heads of educational institutions which tend to complain most loudly about being overregulated, lobby the hardest for more federal subsidies whose receipt subjects them to ever tighter control.

In recent decades the purposes of regulation were enormously expanded—for environmental and health protection, greater safety, civil rights and just social engineering. Regulatory action by government virtually exploded in the 1970s. The *Federal Register* which publishes all new regulations grew from 2355 pages in 1936 to 10,528 in 1956, to 20,036 in 1970 and to 87,012 in 1980.

The American public's attitude is somewhat ambivalent, shifting between "there ought to be a law" and "nobody can tell me what to do—this is a free country." Most public opinion polls show a bare majority of those opposing *more* regulation over those favoring it. The relative popularity of much of current regulation derives from the fact that hardly anybody knows what it really costs him.

Expenditures of 57 federal regulatory agencies jumped from $0.9 billion in 1970 to $6.0 billion in 1980, their staff from 27,661 to about 90,000. But that is barely the tip of the iceberg because compliance costs are borne by the affected industries. Total cost of regulation may be twenty times as high as federal outlays according to estimates by Murray L. Weidenbaum, director of the Center for the Study of American Business at Washington University, St. Louis, who has studied the costs of regulations and the potential of reform more thoroughly than anyone else. He put total cost in 1980 at $126 billion.[16]

Most people applaud when a government agency mandates the installation and operation of facilities which are believed to improve the environment, health or safety. Who could oppose such action, particularly when its cost is placed on the industry, on big corporations, on the "fat cats"? But in the end, neither management nor the stockholders pay for all this. Consumers will pay, complaining about exorbitant prices, but not knowing why they went sky-high.

Costs of regulation go far beyond mere cash outlays. Many activities are not undertaken because they would no longer be economical or funds are unavailable. A business may not be started, a new product not researched and developed, a plant not built or enlarged, thousands of workers not hired, because the funds had to be used to pay for a mandated facility or the prices that would have to be charged would make the product noncompetitive.

The avalanche of regulatory orders in the 1970s bears a substantial share of the responsibility for the drop in productivity growth from an average 3% annually, 1960 to 1973, to *negative* growth, i.e., a net decline of output per man-hour in 1978, 1979 and 1980. That contributed materially to soaring inflation rates.

Much of the cost of regulation cannot be measured at this time though it is substantial. Some of our products can no longer meet foreign competition because of labor regulations. That may mean smaller exports, larger imports and fewer jobs for American workers. Affirmative action means that employers can no longer hire and promote to supervisory positions the applicants and workers whom they deem to be the most competent and productive. The morale of the staff and the work crews suffers when consideration of demonstrated effort and performance must take second place in determining awards. If banks and other moneylenders can no longer exercise their judgment on the creditworthiness of applicants and must extend credit to risks they would regard marginal, increased delinquencies will exert upward pressure on interest rates. Inventory losses through pilferage have been soaring since stores and employers generally can no longer apply the safeguards, tests, preventive measures they once used to keep such losses to a minimum. The new federal bankruptcy law that took effect in October 1979 makes it much easier for debtors to declare themselves bankrupt and protects them more effectively from their creditors. It also will make credit less available and far more expensive. The list of governmental intrusions which boost costs could be continued and is virtually endless.

The results of cost-benefit analysis are not always definitive or clear-cut because some of the facts essential to a comprehensive appraisal are not readily available and some of them depend on value judgments. A raise in minimum wages will boost the income of many low-income persons. But others will lose their jobs—or not be hired—because the cost of employing them will be greater than the value of their output. Their job may be automated or their service or product may be priced out of the market and discontinued.

Occasionally cost considerations may sway Congress. Construction of the $120 million Tellico Dam was halted by a federal court just before completion in 1977 when it was found that the dam might endanger the snail darter, a newly discovered 3-inch fish whose existence had not even been known. That the dam would produce enough electricity to save nearly half a million barrels of oil a year did not impress the court, but caused Congress to pass a special exemption from the Endangered Species Act which President Carter "with regret" did not veto.

Findings by the Congressional Budget Office that compliance with a demand by the Department of Transportation to install lifts for wheelchairs on buses, room for wheelchairs on all railroad cars and elevators in subway and rail stations will cost $38 per ride, has not yet led to a change in the requirement, though the *New York Times* editorially asked, "Must Every Bus Kneel to the Disabled?" (November 18, 1979) and the *Wall Street Journal* criticized "the regulatory mentality that converts a compassionate impulse into an economic monstrosity" ("Ruthless Compassion," September 29, 1979). The *swine flu* debacle in 1976 which caused thousands of claims for damages totaling several billions is an example of regulatory ambition gone mad that should long be remembered.

The issue is not whether regulation is necessary but how far it should go. Enthusiasts are trying to build a *riskless society* and Congress, swayed by emotional arguments, lost a sense of proportion. Henry Fairlie once commented: "With Ralph Nader at the head of a wagon train, no one would have made it across the plains, none would have crossed the Rockies and no immigrant would have pushed noisomely out of the gutter."

Well-intentioned though much of the regulatory wave of the 1970s was, its overall burden turned out to be more than the American economy can bear—even now when we have not yet shouldered all of the long-range costs. There must be a thorough and painstaking review with a broad counterwave in the early 1980s with the goal of *deregulation*. Cost analysis needs to play a major role in that endeavor.

But a good dose of plain common sense—which was manifestly lacking in the 1960s and 1970s—could prove eminently beneficial.

Inflation—A Tool of the Wayward Welfare State

Inflation has been so much in the center of public interest for well over a decade, that an enormous and growing literature on the subject has been piling up on our library shelves. I could not possibly, within the framework of this book, adequately cover all the manifold ramifications of inflation. But neither can I omit a discussion of the relationship between inflation and the welfare state and their impact on each other. High-rate inflation, as is now widely recognized, is largely a result of American welfare state policies in recent decades. But it also serves, as has not been made clear in most of the literature, as an instrument for accomplishing redistributive goals of today's welfare state. I shall attempt, as compactly as I can, to sketch, in terms of shirt-sleeve economics, the causes and effects of our seemingly irrepressible inflation and outline minimum requirements for ending it.

U.S. Presidents have long been denouncing inflation in the strongest terms they could find in their dictionaries—from Dwight Eisenhower who called inflation "a robber and a thief" at a time when it was running well below two percent a year, to Jimmy Carter who declared inflation fighting "the moral equivalent of war" when its rate had quadrupled, and, to Ronald Reagan whose overwhelming victory in November 1980 was at least in part due to the public's unhappiness with double-digit rates during the Carter regime, and to expectations that a Reagan administration would do better.

Despite the anti-inflationary oratory of presidents and congressional leaders, prices kept soaring between 1965 and 1980, with but few short-lived relapses. Prospects for 1981 appear no better and opinion polls suggest that the public expects inflation to get worse, though government leaders have consistently predicted and promised lower rates.

Does not *anybody* know how to reduce inflation? The fact is, we know. There is no secret or mystery about running an inflation-free economy—the answer can be found in most standard economic texts. It can also be found by studying history which reveals that many countries, including the United States, experienced very little, if any, inflation for long periods, except in wartime, *prior to the coming of the*

70

welfare state. The inflation rate averaged 2.1% annually between 1900 and 1965—only 1.3% between 1960 and 1965. It started climbing after enactment of the Great Society programs and reached 13.3% in 1979. Military spending played no part in this: it dropped from 9.2% of GNP in 1960 to 5.1% in 1979.

According to public opinion polls, a majority of the American people believe that inflation could be reduced or eliminated through mandatory price controls. To the average consumer, inflation means that stores and other businesses raise prices, usually to make bigger profits. The simplest way to stop them from doing so, many consumers believe, is a government edict to freeze prices at their current level. That belief manifests nothing as clearly as the level of economic education, or any education, most of our schools provide for their students.

Price control may work, more or less, for a short period; but in the long run it is like clamping a lid on a pot of boiling water. If you turn off the heat, the lid will keep the water from spilling over. But if you leave the heat on, the lid will blow or the pot will explode.

The debate hinges mostly on: will controls work? Historical records on this are quite clear: they won't, at least not for very long, unless certain other steps are taken to keep prices from rising. And if they are, there may be no need for controls. Many rulers have been trying to decree maximum prices, with examples going back up to four thousand years. But even the most draconic sanctions were not able to restrain prices for very long in the presence of continued economic pressures and debasement of the currency. Most economists now recognize that price controls create scarcities and lower quality. Controls may serve as a temporary expedient while effective measures are being taken to end the upward trend in prices; few economists now regard price control an adequate remedy for inflation.

Guidelines and similar appeals to voluntary compliance have failed every time they were tried. Civic spirit will not prevail when people recognize that few will heed such appeals for long, and that "jawboning" will prove as effective as King Cole's command to the waves to subside. After all, government itself is responsible for inflation and only government can end it.

Inflation has lasted in the United States for fifteen years, and has been growing worse, because we have been living—or trying to live—beyond our means. Now we are looking for a painless way to continue living in the manner to which we would like to become accustomed. But there is no "ouchless" way of returning to a balanced and sound economy.

In conducting counterinflationary programs, our decision makers have been acting like some persons who would like to lose weight: they know that they ought to stick to a slim diet. But they can't resist the temptation of the many goodies within reach.

The fight against inflation can be won only if it is granted top priority in decisions on public policy. But, contrary to much oratory, it is not. The goals of the wayward welfare state continued to rank tops in the 1960s and 1970s and they determined the outcome.

The seven-member Board of Governors of the Federal Reserve System, appointed by the President for overlapping 14-year terms, but not subject to his command, regulates the supply of money and credit. It has been trying to keep supply "tight," responding to trends and needs of the economy. But no more than central banks in other countries, can the "Fed" long refuse to meet the financial needs of the government. Action to keep the magnitude of those needs under control must be taken *before* commitments are made and *not when the bills are due.*

Monetarists are correct in saying that inflation can be prevented or stopped by restraining the creation of money and credit, and in no other way. But experience has shown that for practical political reasons, the brakes must be applied much earlier, at the time when the fiscal plans are made. Otherwise, the accumulated momentum may become irresistible and eventually sweep even the most determined Federal Reserve Board. The board is very lonely, devoid of a sizable constituency to rush to its support when it is under attack. When the United States Government needs dozens of billions to meet its obligations, when cries—or roars and threats—are coming from all over the country that unbearably high interest rates and unavailability of credit are paralyzing the economy, throwing thousands of firms into bankruptcy and condemning millions of workers to idleness, the board is up against the wall. In the end, the board's defenses are pierced and the banknote press is called into action. Money may or may not be the root of all evil. But too much of it in circulation surely is the root of all inflation.

Business firms, workers, consumers alike feel that more money helps them to meet the problem of inflation. But every economist knows that more money is not the answer to the problem of inflation. *It is the problem.*

It has been said that budget deficits by themselves do not cause prices to rise and that elimination of deficits would not end the upward trend. That is quite true. Other fuels also fire the engines of inflation. But the chances of cutting inflation rates, by any conceivable means, at a time when federal budget deficits equal 2% or more of GNP—they actually averaged 2.3% of GNP over the past six years—are slim. Several other forces are at work generating high-rate inflation and they all must be weakened or neutralized if prices are to be prevented from continuing their upward surge.

A reduction of federal spending, not necessarily of dollar amounts but as a percentage of GNP, is an indispensable part of an anti-inflationary program. Federal outlays climbed from 20.5% of GNP in FY 1971 to 23.3% in FY 1981 (estimated). Defense spending fell from 7.3% of GNP to 5.7% while nondefense jumped from 13.2% of GNP to 17.6%. With defense requirements necessarily on the upgrade, the nondefense segment of the federal budget, whose share rose from 64% in 1971 to 76% in 1981 seems the natural candidate for cutbacks. But how are we going to hang the bell around the cat's neck? While about three-fourths of total federal outlays are labeled "uncontrollable," i.e., not subject to the reductions by the president and the Congress through the budgetary process, nearly 90% of expenditures for *domestic* purposes are "uncontrollable." This means that the federal budget cannot be cut much through the process instituted by the budget reform enacted in 1974. It can be done only by changing the basic statutes authorizing programs and specifying "entitlements." Appropriations must again establish spending limits.

But even if the nondefense share of the budget can be substantially slimmed from its current 76% of total outlays and 23.3% of GNP—and that is a big IF—price levels may continue to rise unless several other directions are changed. Federal tax and expenditure policies shift huge amounts from savers to consumers. That reduces the funds which otherwise would be available for investment in productive facilities that probably would be more modern and more efficient. Our savings rates have been running between one-half to one-third of those in other advanced countries and our rates of capital formation and industrial investment have also been much lower. The saver-to-consumer shift inflates consumer demand which in turn exerts an upward push on prices.

Federal regulation of industrial and business activities multiplied in the 1970s and thereby added enormous amounts to the cost basis while

73

lowering productivity. Annual growth in output per man-hour used to average about 3 percent or more and turned negative in 1978, 1979 and 1980. Taking 1967 as 100, manufacturing productivity stood in 1979 at 129.2 in the United States, at an average of 201.9 in ten major industrial countries. Quality and morale of the American labor force have suffered in consequence of government intervention. But organized labor in the United States continues to demand wage boosts, which, in the absence of commensurate productivity increases, raise per unit labor costs. Unit labor costs rose by 101% between 1970 and 1980, consumer prices by 110%. This means that the relation between labor costs and productivity alone explains most of the rise in consumer prices.

This does not imply that labor started inflation and is responsible for most of it. The major share of the increase in the average weekly wage in the private nonagricultural industry from $120 in 1970 to $232 in 1980 came about in response to higher prices—workers trying to keep up with inflation to maintain living standards. But, absent a commensurate rise in productivity, higher wages add to the cost base which, in turn, is then reflected in higher prices. It is that vicious circle—prices pushing up wages and wages pushing up prices—that generated the seemingly unbeatable upward spiral. The question is not whether the chicken came first or the egg, but who gets to keep the egg. While labor may not have started the inflationary spiral, it did wind up with the egg.

Disproportionate wage boosts, especially in the heavy industries, year after year, are a major cause of persistent high-rate inflation, though none of the political parties or leaders dare recognize this publicly.

DIVISION OF NATIONAL INCOME, 1950 and 1980

	1950	1980	Increase
Employees	65.2%	75.3%	+ 10.1%
Proprietors and corporate profits	30.6	14.7	− 15.9
Interest and rental income	4.2	10.0	+ 5.8
	100.0%	100.0%	0

SOURCES: *Economic Report of the President*, January 1981, pp 254–55; and *Economic Indicators*, February 1981.

The entrepreneurs' share was cut into half over the past three decades, with two-thirds of the difference going to labor, one-third to interest and rental income.

Peter F. Drucker of the Claremont Graduate School recently pointed out that

> it is rapidly becoming clear that both productivity and capital formation depend heavily on the "labor-income ratio"—the proportion of value added, paid out in wages and fringe benefits—and that this is true whether we are talking about a company, an industry or a national economy. If the ratio goes above a certain threshold, apparently between 80% and 85%, productivity declines and capital formation falls too low to maintain jobs, let alone create new ones. [17]

The American economy has not yet reached that level—though its corporate sector is uncomfortably close to it—and still is creating jobs at a good rate. But its capital formation is too low and its productivity in a deep slump. Moreover, the United States now has the world's shortest workweek with an average of 35.6 hours, shrinking at the rate of 1.5 hours a decade. This compares with a workweek of 41.9 hours in West Germany, 41.2 hours in France, 40.7 hours in Japan and 44.5 hours in Switzerland. Small wonder that we have to pay the price for more leisure, rising wages and an increasing overburden of government regulation in the form of high-rate inflation.

The economic function of prices in a free market is to maintain a balance between supply and demand. Higher prices discourage consumption and encourage production and thus work to restore an equilibrium between them. But most people are not willing to lower their consumption and feel that by getting higher wages they can offset higher prices and thus avoid reducing their living standards. That may work all right for an individual. But when everybody gets in the act and manages to boost his income, the imbalance between supply and demand is recreated, prices are forced up another notch, and the spiral continues *ad infinitum.*

If the price of a particular commodity—such as crude oil as a result of OPEC action—multiplies, we must somehow offset the drain, by consuming less either of that particular commodity or of other goods. If, however, government intervenes and tries to enable us to maintain our accustomed level of consumption, the additional money fed into the economy will drive up the general price level, which is exactly what has been happening since 1974.

Under Keynesian theories which dominated public policies and, to a large extent, public opinion, for about four decades, economic stagnation and unemployment are caused by inadequate demand. This can be made up by government infusing more money into the economy which it is hoped will then perk up. It was assumed that there is a trade-off between unemployment and inflation, as illustrated in the Phillips curve. There is supposed to be no danger of inflation at a time of high unemployment. Thus government can expand the money supply, feed funds into the economy, without having to fear inordinate price boosts. Even if prices then moved up slightly, this would be amply offset by the benefits of lower unemployment.

That trade-off never worked too well and broke down in the 1970s: government action to lower unemployment was followed by high inflation rates. It was called stagflation.

What causes stagflation? Some might say that progress in economic science and refinement of political techniques now permit us to enjoy unemployment and inflation simultaneously. If the labor market were free, the presence of economic stagnation and a surplus of job seekers might cause wage rates to yield, thereby reducing production costs and making a rise in the price level unlikely. But wages no longer are flexible nor respond to downward economic fluctuations. Wage rates are protected against an adverse market by cartelization—national, regional, local—in unions that exercise and exploit their monopoly position. That is why wages do not decline, even at times of high unemployment, but continue on an upward trend. Antitrust statutes prevent business from engaging in price fixing but they do not apply to labor. Moreover, even extended periods of idleness are not too uncomfortable if unemployment compensation benefits are reasonably attractive. That makes it easier for organized labor to "hold out." Consequently, governmental action to compensate for economic slack now generates inflationary trends, which in earlier days would not have occurred at a time when the economy was less than buoyant.

Government now tries to protect American workers against foreign competition by various types of import restrictions which force higher prices on American consumers. Laid-off workers in industries affected by foreign competition receive additional benefits from the federal government (trade adjustment assistance) which may cost over $3 billion in 1981. That protects workers in industries whose pay scales are disproportionately high, such as in steel, autos, rubber, from the economic consequences of exacting wages not justified by their productivity. Company losses are made bearable by tax offsets and, if necessary, by a federal bailout. The consumer bears the burden of the taxes as well as of higher prices for American products.

More than a third of Americans are now protected against inflation, wholly or partially, by an indexing of their wages, social benefits, pensions, etc. Many others who are not covered by scheduled indexing receive increases loosely geared to the consumer price index (CPI). This takes much of the sting out of steadily rising prices and substantially softens the vigor with which those affected oppose policies which perpetuate inflation.

The number of Americans who profit handsomely from inflation is widely underestimated. About two-thirds of all families now live in their own home. Suppose a family bought a house for $50,000 in 1970 and paid $10,000 down. Home values multiplied better than two and a half times during the 1970s so that the house might now be worth $150,000. The value of the original equity thus jumped from $10,000 to $110,000, a spectacular gain which gives the family a "net worth" far higher than it could have expected when it bought the house ten years earlier. Supposing the original mortgage equaled 2–1/2 times the family's annual earnings in 1970. By 1980 the mortgage's value (disregarding what may have been paid in principal during the 1970s) may be close to or equal to annual family earnings. Monthly payments may have absorbed 25% of annual family income in 1970; by 1980 they may have equaled only 12% of earnings or less.

Homeownership turned out to be an enormously profitable operation—which explains why so many more entered the housing market and, in the process, drove up the price of homes far ahead of the CPI. This pushed some others out of the housing market unless they were able to participate in one of the government subsidy programs. Most of the gains accrued to the middle class, not to persons in the lowest brackets. Part of the corresponding loss also fell on the middle class, on those who were lenders (investors) rather than borrowers. To some extent this was a huge intergenerational shift in asset holdings—from an older generation investing its savings, to the next generation entering the housing market or moving up in it.

Within ten years, between 1970 and 1980, those who furnished the mortgage funds—through financial intermediaries or directly—saw about half the value of their investments evaporate. Even within the middle class, this probably amounted to a downward shift of wealth, from the more affluent to the less affluent. But primarily it added up to a huge redistribution of income and wealth from the high economic strata to lower strata, entirely attributable to inflation. Homeowners' mortgage debt, estimated at $750 billion and installment and other consumer debt at $400 billion, for a total of $1.15 trillion currently depreciates at over one percent a month. This means a $150 billion annual relief for borrowers and an annual loss of equal size to lenders.

How well do other wealth owners fare? Shares listed on the New York Stock Exchange were valued at $961 billion in 1979. The Dow-Jones industrial index stood at 910 in 1965—and again in July 1980. But the 1980 dollar was worth only 38 cents in terms of the 1965 dollar which means that the average stockholder lost 62% of his holdings. Bonds listed on the exchange totaled $526 billion. At an inflation rate of 13%, the holders of those stocks and bonds lose about $195 billion a year. Total money stocks and liquid assets can be defined in various terms, commonly labeled M1, M2, M3 or L. The most comprehensive measure, "L", totaled $2,372 billion, in December 1980. At the current rate of inflation securities owners lose about $500 billion of their assets each year. Inflation could also be viewed as a tax on all wealth except real estate, jewelry, art, foreign holdings, etc., which is currently levied at the rate of about one percent per month.

Since persons in the lower economic brackets own very little, if any, of the monetary assets, inflation amounts largely to a gradual expropriation of the "haves." While social security benefits are indexed to the CPI, few of the other (private) annuities and pensions or insurance contracts are. Therefore, their value constantly shrinks. An annual decline of 13% means a loss of 45 cents on each dollar within five years, of 70 cents within ten years, of 83 cents within fifteen years, and of 95 cents within twenty-five years. This amounts to nearly total confiscation within one generation.

To be sure, much of the wealth held in the top brackets consists of real estate which, from past experience, appreciates even when expressed in *constant* dollars. But real estate also probably is the most widely—some would say most democratically—distributed form of property. Fifty million American families live in their own homes and they have, on the average, been doing very well, as I showed earlier.

What all of this adds up to is a fact which much of the abundant literature on inflation has avoided mentioning: *inflation is an engine of downward redistribution of wealth and income which has proven enormously effective over the past fifteen years.* Such redistribution is precisely the goal of the egalitarian drive which is carried into practice by today's American welfare state. Anti-inflationary action, widely proclaimed by political leaders as their foremost aim, was bound to fail because, if allowed to succeed, it would have sharply reduced the effectiveness of the overriding priority of income redistribution.

This explains why left of center politicians and economists have almost always advocated policies which tend to raise rather than lower inflation rates. When public sentiment against ever-rising prices turned into a national consensus, even spokesmen for the left felt impelled to pay lip service to anti-inflationary goals. But they focused on means on how to live with inflation more than on ways to end it. They proposed techniques by which persons in the lower brackets could be insulated against higher prices, generally through CPI-related escalator clauses. They advocated more extensive indexing for the "have-nots" so that most of the burden of inflation could be loaded on the "haves," persons in the higher economic strata. That paves the way to their gradual expropriation. Harvard sociologist Christopher Jencks summed it up succinctly: "Why worry about inflation? The big losers, after all, are the rich.

Why don't the rich fight inflation more strongly? Some of them escape from its depredations by concentrating their assets in real estate and other inflation-proof forms while keeping their dollar holdings on the negative, i.e., debt side. Many others immensely enjoy seeing their net worth cross the magical line of seven digits—who would not like to become a millionaire?—and others are delighted at adding more millions to those they have—closing their eyes to the fact that much of their added wealth is but an inflation-caused illusion.

Inflation and other redistributive policies bear much of the responsibility for the low rates of savings, capital formation, industrial investment, lagging productivity in the United States. They also account for our poor rate of economic expansion in recent years. The political left has never been as eager to promote economic growth as in cutting itself a bigger slice of the pie. Nor has it displayed as much interest in giving to the poor as in taking from the rich. On the whole, it has been successful for quite some time. What it should remember is that only a very rich nation, whose wealth keeps growing, has much to redistribute. There is such a thing as killing the goose that lays the golden eggs.

79

If the policies and trends of the 1970s are permitted to continue indefinitely they will lead us on the historical path to hyperinflation. From double-digit rates per year we may progress to double-digit rates per month, per week, per day. That is precisely what happened at some time or other in China, in France, in Germany, in Hungary and elsewhere.

It can't happen here? Of course, it can't—just as surely as the Titanic was unsinkable.

How can inflationary trends be reversed? Above all, by focusing on how to *add* to the nation's wealth rather than on how to *redistribute* it more effectively. Here are some specific policies toward that end.

1. Government spending must be reduced to a lower percentage of GNP and kept within revenues. With defense requiring a growing share, if accumulated military deficiencies are to be remedied, this calls for rather severe restraint on the biggest and fastest growing of our domestic, i.e., social programs.

2. Money and credit must be tightly and consistently controlled, regardless of outcries about excessive interest rates and painful credit restrictions.

3. Tax and expenditure policies must focus on incentives for savings, capital formation, enterprise and investment rather than on redistribution and consumption.

4. Government regulation of business must pass the test of strict cost-benefit analysis and be limited to what the economy can bear without unduly reducing productivity growth.

5. Government must adopt a more evenhanded policy in the treatment of management and labor, and refrain from one-sided intervention in contract negotiations, despite the obvious discrepancy in their relative voting power.

Many Unhappy Returns

That taxes are too heavy is a perennial and justified complaint that in itself proves little. If a majority of the American people truly felt that taxes are oppressive and ought to be reduced, they could do something about it, in a system of free government. They could elect representatives who run on a platform of lower taxes and defeat candidates who advocate bigger spending programs for governmental services and more generous benefits. Though the outright proponents of higher taxes, such as John Kenneth Galbraith and his followers, are distinctly in the minority, the spokesmen for more liberal public programs seem to swing enough weight to have been successful in their drive over the past quarter century. All governmental revenues (federal, state, local) tripled, in *constant* dollars, between 1952 and 1978 while the nation's income and product (GNP) slightly more than doubled (+135%). As a result, governmental receipts increased from 29.6% of GNP to 36.5%, making the burden about one-fifth heavier.

The weight and growth of the tax load was in recent decades widely attributed to the demands of the military. But this is contradicted by the fact that national defense outlays dropped from 49.2% of all government expenditures in 1952 to 15.9% in 1978, and from 13.3% of GNP to 5.1%. Thus we are now devoting a far smaller share of our income to our national security than we did.

Moreover: federal revenues remained quite stable in relationship to income—21.2% of GNP in 1952, 21.4% in 1978. Federal income tax rates were cut several times to offset the impact of inflation on a progressive tax system. But the state and local tax load nearly doubled—from 8.4% of GNP to 15.1%—to multiply funds for education, welfare and other domestic services. Steady rounds of tax boosts multiplied receipts from state and local income taxes nearly tenfold (in *constant* dollars), from consumption taxes (mostly on retail sales) fourfold, on property threefold. Taxpayers have a more direct say on their state and local taxes than they have on federal taxes and they approved or acquiesced in most of the tax boosts by affirmative votes on tax and bond proposals at the ballot box.

In the later 1970s the steady rise in state and local taxes slowed down and ground to a halt. A local drive in California in the spring of 1978 led to adoption of proposition #13 which cut property taxes in half. That inspired similar movements in other states, some of which led to restraints on state and local taxes. Several legislatures and local authorities heeded the warning and lowered tax rates so as to take the steam out of the popular tax cut drive. State and local tax receipts actually dropped between 1978 and 1980, when measured in *constant* dollars or as a percentage of GNP. Alarmed by the passage of proposition #13 and of other tax restrictions elsewhere, organizations with a stake or interest in expansion of public services mounted a counterattack. By more effective political strategy or sheer numbers, they beat the tax cutters. Proposition #9 in June 1980 which would have halved California income taxes lost at the polls and several comparable proposals in other states did not fare well at the November 1980 elections. The long predicted tax revolt, viewed by some with hope, by others as a threat, fizzled within two years of its initial triumph. Spending forces turned out to be stronger and better organized than their opponents. Prospects for substantial state and local tax cuts no longer look as promising as they once did.

The taxes which the American people pay to their governments are not extraordinarily high compared with the load borne by the citizens of other industrial nations. Related to income, the tax burden in Holland and the Scandinavian countries is 50% higher than in the United States, in Germany, Austria, France, Belgium and Great Britain about 25% higher. This does not seem to have adversely affected their rate of economic progress in recent decades, compared with the United States. It is commonly agreed that heavy taxes deter and impede economic expansion but there is only sketchy evidence to prove it. Some countries with high levels of taxation and liberal programs of social insurance have achieved remarkable rates of economic growth and high per capita incomes.

It could well be that the *form* of taxation has a greater impact on the rate of economic development than its overall *magnitude*.

It is well known that the American tax structure is unique. No other industrial country has a tax system that is so heavily biased in favor of consumption and against capital formation, in a determined attempt to redistribute income. Most major countries use a consumption tax as a mainstay of their revenue system; the United States is the only country that does not use such a tax at all at the national level. Nor do other countries rely for their revenue as heavily on income taxes as does the United States.

The individual income tax, since 1965 graduated from 14 to 70 percent, is by far the biggest single tax, yielding well over a quarter of a trillion dollars a year. It is the pride and joy of those who see in it a major and effective tool for making progress toward their egalitarian goals. They do attack the income tax because it contains many "loopholes" which, it is asserted, enable many wealthy persons to escape bearing their fair share—or any share—of the tax burden. Examination shows that the individual income tax is indeed full of loopholes.

Someone once well defined a loophole as a provision in the tax code from which the particular speaker—or the group he represents—derives either no or not enough benefits.

82

Less than half of all personal income, as defined in national income accounts, is subject to the rate scale of the federal income tax. Untaxed income totaled more than one trillion dollars in 1979, with most of it accruing to persons in the lower-middle, and low-income brackets. Little of the untaxed income is in the high brackets. The biggest "loopholes" which account for most of the untaxed income were in 1978: 220 million personal exemptions. At the $1,000 rate effective from January 1979 on they amount to $220 billion; standard deductions—renamed in 1977 zero bracket amounts—$216 billion; itemized deductions $164 billion ($60 billion state-local taxes, $61 billion interest paid, $20 billion charitable donations, $23 billion medical and other deductions) of which $76 billion were offset in zero bracket amounts, leaving *net* deductions of $88 billion; social welfare payments $220 billion. These four items thus account for about three-fourths of the untaxed personal income.

In 1974 Congress renamed tax loopholes "tax expenditures" and ordered the amounts to be shown in each year's budget. The budget's warning that "adding together separate tax expenditures would be misleading" was widely disregarded and one compilation asserted that in 1981 "tax breaks added up to $229 billion a year." The implication intended, and sometimes expressed, that government could collect those funds from the special beneficiaries if tax expenditures were eliminated and that most or a sizable share of the amounts go to business is wrong. The bulk of tax expenditures redounds to persons in the lower- and middle-income brackets. The biggest of them are: employer contributions for employee fringe benefits (mostly medical and retirement) $41 billion; deductibility of homeowners' mortgage interest and property taxes $28 billion; deductibility of other state and local taxes $18 billion; deductibility of charitable contributions $10 billion; nontaxability of social security, unemployment compensation and similar social benefits $24 billion.

Tax expenditure amounts shown in the budget are purely hypothetical, computed as if taxpayers engaged in such activities, regardless of whether they are taxed or not. The fact is that Congress enacted those provisions after due deliberation and mostly for the explicit purpose of making certain desirable activities economically feasible and promoting their expansion. If those provisions were repealed many of the activities would collapse. Repeal of many others would be tantamount to huge general tax boosts.

It would be much more informative for the public if instead of computing tax expenditures, the Internal Revenue Service disclosed each year the total amount of personal income not taxed by the federal government, broken down by income brackets and by the amount accounted for by each of the major provisions.

Charges that tax expenditures are largely benefits for business and the rich recall the parable of the man who decried the mote in somebody else's eye but could not see the beam in his own. To be sure, there are some tax "shelters" protecting or favoring certain economic activities, usually for reasons which Congress carefully considered before approving a tax concession. Capital gains rates have been bitterly attacked as unfairly giving advantages to stock speculators and the wealthy over the working man. But to tax long-term capital gains as if they were current income would be the most effective way to freeze investments and bring the country's economy to a screeching halt. The United States once tried, for several years, to tax capital gains as regular income and found out that this is counterproductive.

It has long been recognized that growth in productivity and in the economy depend on effective incentives for investment in technological advance and expansion. Beginning with investment tax credits in 1962, a few steps were taken in that direction. A shift in recent years among professional economists and the public from demand-side economics—better known as Keynesianism—to supply-side economics brought a great deal of lip service from policymakers but little effective action.

Whenever tax cuts were under consideration, political leaders emphasized relief for persons in the lower brackets while shifting more of the burden to taxpayers at higher income levels. They view redistribution of income as the prime purpose of taxation and of government generally. That is why they focus more on how to slice the pie than on baking a bigger pie.

Millions of income earners were freed of any income tax liability in recent decades and thereby also freed of concern about the size and growth of federal spending. On last account, the top 12% of taxpayers paid more than half the federal income tax and the top half paid over 90%. Most of the social security tax boost effective in 1979, the biggest tax boost in U.S. history, was placed on earners in the higher brackets. That egalitarian policy of a welfare state running wild is popular with its beneficiaries and may sometimes pay off in votes. But

84

by further diminishing financial incentives for greater efforts by our most productive people, it slows economic growth.

If all personal income were taxed, eliminating exemptions, exclusions, deductions, and credits, income tax rates could be cut to half and still yield the same revenue. A flat income tax of 10% to 11% on *all* personal income would bring in about as much money as the current 14% to 70% scale with its thousands of "loopholes." In all likelihood, it would bring in more, by stimulating individual initiative and economic growth. What represses motivation and expansion is not the average tax rate, which is merely a statistical concept, but the marginal tax rate which deters individuals from exerting greater efforts. But proposals to lower high marginal rates invariably are opposed as favoring the rich, as "Robin Hood in reverse" policies. This is why plans to tax *all* income at low flat rates are politically unrealistic and not likely to materialize in the near future. A most effective way of stimulating economic growth would be a reduced reliance on the income tax and the adoption of an expenditures tax. By leaving savings free of tax, we could encourage capital formation and industrial expansion. This would help solve several of our economic problems simultaneously.

The United States levies a higher corporate profits tax than any other country, although that tax is probably the economically most damaging tax in our system. Not because it taxes the stockholder, as is widely believed, but because it punishes the efficient producer, restricts industrial expansion, penalizes capital formation, and adversely affects our competitiveness in international trade. Its immense political appeal has prevented even a partial replacement of the corporate profits tax with a value-added tax that has become a main revenue source for most major European countries.

The role of the corporate tax has declined, from 28% of all tax revenues in 1952 to 15% in 1978. This was due to the elimination of the excess profits tax in 1954, a reduction in the corporate tax rate from 52% to 48%, and a significant shift in the division of national income from ownership (and corporate profits) to employee compensation. Investment in corporate ownership has become less attractive: the Dow-Jones industrial stock index, when expressed in *constant* dollars, lost nearly two-thirds between 1965 and 1980. That expresses and reflects, more clearly than any other single indicator, the ill-treatment of corporate enterprise in recent decades. Corporate profits dropped from 12.5% of national income in 1952 to 10.6% in 1978 and to 8.6% in 1980. Effective in 1979, corporate tax rates were slightly reduced, especially for companies with a profit below $100,000. Total receipts are expected to shrink to 9% of all federal revenues by 1982. A shrinking role of corporate taxation may help to reduce the adverse impact of our tax structure. But major improvements in the American economy are unlikely to occur unless our "soak the rich" policy of exploiting corporations is replaced by a program of viewing and treating them as the most effective instrument of economic expansion.

No tax has been on the receiving end of as many vituperative attacks for as long a time as the property tax; to some extent, for good reasons. But great progress has been made in recent decades in improving the assessment process and administration in general. Exemptions may be too generous in some states, but they average only about one-third of the base, compared with one-half the base on the federal individual income tax. Whatever its shortcomings may be, the property tax is the mainstay of local government, which could hardly maintain some semblance of autonomy without an independent source of revenue. There is no substitute for the property tax, without which the remnants of home rule of local communities would largely disappear from the American scene.

Estimates in the federal budget for FY 1982 envisage an increase in receipts from $402 billion in 1978 to $712 billion in 1982. Such a $310 billion boost in federal revenues would raise the tax burden by the equivalent of 2.8% of GNP and have a depressing impact on the nation's economy. Because of our income tax structure and simultaneous inflation, tax liabilities have consistently been rising faster than personal income and the burden became heavier every year. To offset such automatic tax boosts Congress has been authorizing income tax cuts at periodic intervals—the last time in 1978—and thereby kept the federal tax burden at an approximately even level for over a quarter century. In the later part of 1980 a national consensus seemed to develop that the time had again come for substantial tax relief, especially on the federal income tax.

Federal receipts from the income tax rose from $181 billion in 1978 to $284 billion in 1981, an average of $34 billion a year. This suggests that an annual income tax cut of 10% would just about offset the automatic increase. Such a cut would equal 1% of GNP, and, if continued for three years, ·compensate for the above mentioned increase in the federal tax burden equal to 2.8% of GNP between 1978 and 1982.

Several other factors, however, must be considered. Federal tax receipts have for over a decade been insufficient to meet expenditures, with the deficit amounting to $60 billion in 1980 and probably no less in 1981. Federal expenditures rose at an annual average of $70 billion between 1978 and 1981.

This means that if federal taxes are to be cut to prevent the burden from continuing to rise and to reduce it to the level that prevailed until 1978, expenditures will have to be cut very substantially. While tax relief may cause the economy to expand and thereby swell federal tax receipts, a continuation of current spending trends would result in continued huge budgetary deficits. Sizable expenditure cuts will not be easy to accomplish, but they are imperative if taxes are to be eased.

If tax cuts are to yield maximum benefit by stimulating and producing faster economic growth, they will have to be in the nature of tax reform to balance our lopsided tax structure. By moderating redistributive and economically counterproductive features, neutrality could become the goal of American tax policy.

Crime Without Punishment

For decades dozens of experts and official commissions have been telling us that the appalling growth of crime is a function and result of neglect of the disadvantaged and oppressed in our society and that the nation has only itself to blame for the consequences of its stinginess in the treatment of the unfortunate in our midst. President Johnson's *Commission on Law Enforcement and the Administration of Justice* concluded:

> Reducing poverty, discrimination, ignorance, disease and urban blight, and the anger, cynicism or despair those conditions can inspire, is one great step toward reducing crime . . . .
>
> Warring on poverty, inadequate housing and unemployment, is warring on crime. A civil rights law is a law against crime. Money for schools is money against crime. Medical, psychiatric, and family-counseling are services against crime.

That sounds reasonable. Here is the record: Over the past quarter century government outlays for income support through dozens of public assistance and other social welfare programs multiplied eightfold in *constant* dollars, and tripled as a percentage of national income and product (GNP); the percentage of persons officially classified as having a cash income below the poverty level—not counting food stamps and other in-kind benefits—was cut in half; funds for public education multiplied three times—on a per student basis in *constant* dollars—and length of school attendance increased; several civil rights laws were enacted and are being enforced; medical programs for the indigent multiplied to a point where poor people now average more physician contacts annually than persons at higher income levels; the percentage of "substandard" housing dropped to a fraction, according to Census surveys.

What did those efforts produce? A fivefold multiplication in the number of serious crimes ("index crimes") over the past two decades during which the country's population grew merely 28%. Predatory street crime is rampant, fear stalks our cities and few feel safe in their homes.

By the rules of statistics, that adds up to a high correlation between feeding multibillion amounts into social programs and getting a return in the form of an explosion in the crime rate. That is not exactly what the programs' protagonists intended, promised and expected. Nor does it necessarily prove a causal relationship. But it does suggest a high probability of this being no mere coincidence; the dominant idea of its time, the egalitarian spirit of the welfare state run amuck, could be behind both, runaway social spending and multiplying crime.

Traditional alibis for the failure of governmental programs—inadequate appropriations and stinginess in resource allocation—are hard to document in law enforcement. Expenditures for police protection (federal, state, local) jumped from $1.1 billion in 1952 to $12.9 billion in 1978, quintupling in *constant* dollars and doubling as a percentage of GNP. Police employment nearly tripled. There is now one police employee for every 317 persons in the population, compared with a 1:618 ratio in 1952; police departments generally have been supplied with the latest in sophisticated hardware. Defeat in the crime war does not suggest that enforcement personnel was taking it easy and neglecting its responsibilities. The number of policemen murdered in line of duty—1123 over the past decade—testifies to that.

Congress in 1968 established a federal *Law Enforcement Assistance Administration* (LEAA) which in a dozen years spent over $7 billion, with President Nixon in his first term unleashing an anticrime offensive. But the crime rate kept going up. LEAA's apparent ineffectiveness so disillusioned its former supporters that Congress in the fall of 1980 decided to phase out virtually all of the agency's programs.

The failure of the various anticrime campaigns actually is quite easy to explain. Most of today's offenders don't steal bread to feed their families. Nor are they the products of dilapidated and underfinanced schools. Many are professionals who did their research well and learned from it that crime offers a lucrative career with moderate risks. Gradually, the word got around also among less sophisticated would-be criminals: Crime is a profitable and prosperous industry. In a recent book captioned *Crime Pays* Thomas Plate listed criminal "salaries" which, depending on specialty and skill, run from $15,000 to $165,000, on flexible office hours.

Relating the number of reported "index" crimes, now 11 million annually, to the average of 130,000 persons entering federal and state prisons each year, the prospect of *not* going to prison for committing a serious offense averages almost 99 percent. A recent official study found that out of every 100 persons arrested on felony charges in New York City in 1979, 80 were not prosecuted and only one went to prison. Between 1957 and 1977, the number of reported crimes increased nationally by 429%, the number of persons sent to prison by 60%, the size of the prison population by 42%. Thus the likelihood of a criminal's being incarcerated was cut to one-fifth within twenty years. Sending a criminal to prison seems to be going out of style. The percentage of reported crimes which at least resulted in an arrest dropped from 26% in 1961 to 21% in 1978.

The one criminal in about a hundred who is unlucky enough to wind up behind bars, serves, on the average, only half the time to which he was sentenced—usually under conditions which are far less uncomfortable than they were a few decades or generations ago. Is there any other money-making, ego-satisfying enterprise in which the chances are nearly as good? Do we have to look farther for reasons why crime rates continue to soar?

The only way to reduce crime is to make its cost prohibitively high by increasing the certainty and severity of punishment,

    1. by assuring that most offenders are identified and brought to justice;

    2. by shaping the sentence to fit the crime, by making the term actually served long enough to constitute an effective deterrent.

Repeaters should not get an opportunity of again becoming a menace to society.

Deterrence is not as appealing a method as pouring huge amounts into social programs, or attempts at rehabilitation, futile though they have proven to be.

To talk about certainty of punishment at a time when four out of every five offenders are not apprehended, is sheer irony. Nor would it be fair to attribute the sad record of arrests and convictions largely to police incompetency and indolence, although police morale and effectiveness certainly have suffered in recent years from a dilution of employment and promotional tests and a downgrading of objective standards of qualification.

The traditional informality of American life and movements—in contrast to long-established practices in Europe and many other parts of the world—undoubtedly exact a cost in making identification of criminals more difficult and tracing their movements often impossible. This could be remedied only if the American public were willing to accept inconveniences which elsewhere are institutionalized.

The main cause of our low—and declining—arrest rates are the rules with which the courts, and especially the U.S. Supreme Court, have blindfolded and handcuffed our police. The "exclusionary rule"—to which the United States certainly has an exclusive claim—under which many criminals, proven guilty beyond a shadow of doubt, have been acquitted and released, is just one example of a game that is stacked in favor of the offender. The *Miranda*, *Mallory* and *Wade* rules turn the serious business of bringing a criminal to justice into a sportsmanlike competition of wits, with the suspects given an advantage and the prosecution a handicap. That may make proceedings more fascinating to watch—on television or in a courtroom—but does not necessarily advance the ends of justice. The application and results of the "temporary insanity" rule sometimes amount to plain insanity.

Throughout most of the world, law enforcement authorities exercise the powers they need to protect society from assault by evildoers. In the United States police forces have seen themselves increasingly restricted and we are reaping the harvest of showing compassion and respecting the rights of the offender more than of the victim, of accepting excuses for deliberate and violent disregard of essential rules of civil behavior—at a terrible and growing cost, year after year, to millions of innocent people.

90

Most foreign countries forbid their residents to own or carry handguns. In the United States an estimated half of the people have a gun—and feel that they need it because the police too obviously are unable to protect them. A law disallowing guns could not and would not be enforced under current circumstances. It has been said: If guns are outlawed, only outlaws will have guns.

Federal courts bear the major responsibility for the unsafe conditions which now exist in the country. They permit trials to go on for many months in cases which in Britain and other western countries would be concluded within days. They seem to be too concerned about the minutiae of suspects' rights while jeopardizing the rights and security of the defendants' prospective future victims.

This is not to say that legislatures and Congress have done what they could and should do to deter would-be criminals from engaging in acts of violence against peaceful citizens. Congress has been playing around—and I cannot think of a more appropriate term—for fifteen years with a recodification of federal criminal law. The new code was never enacted and with its failure in the fall of 1980 may finally be dead. It would not have provided the necessary improvements but largely reconfirmed the current painfully inadequate law which does not even come near to instituting the needed reforms.

A war on crime to be conducted with any chance of reducing rather than increasing the incidence of offenses against persons and property must be initiated at the federal level. Unless it grants police departments the powers they need to identify and apprehend the offenders, and to secure the necessary evidence, and until it mandates punishment sufficiently severe to deter criminal acts, prospects for improvement are slim indeed.

The Enfeebled Giant

Grave as the threat is from ever growing crime, the most ominous danger to our long-range national survival lies in a gradual weakening of our national defense. From unquestioned supremacy at the end of World War II, our strength and preparedness have fallen to second best in several major military fields and, in the judgment of many experts, in their aggregate power. For the first time in history, there is uncertainty about our ability to defeat any conceivable assault on the United States and its vital interests and doubt about the likelihood that we can incapacitate or destroy an attacker.

Deterrence offers the most potent safeguard against domestic crime or an onslaught from abroad, based on the would-be aggressor's awareness and fear of the consequences, on his knowledge of our capacity and determination to inflict intolerable costs or damage upon him. We fall short on both counts.

With an outlay of $136 billion in FY 1980, certain to rise far above the scheduled $184 billion in FY 1982—probably to over $200 billion—and two million men and women in uniform, our defense establishment offers a mighty and imposing sight. The United States, with a population one-sixth smaller than the Soviet Union's, produces over 70% more in goods and services—combined with its allies three times as much as the USSR and its satellites. It would be militarily more powerful than the Soviet Union if it used its resources and shaped its policy and actions toward that end. But the crucial point is that our adversaries have for many years been building up their war-making potential while ours has been diminishing, measured by the only meaningful yardstick: the combined power we may have to face some day in a major confrontation at a future Armageddon.

That the facade the United States presents is hollow, is suggested by the fact that we have blundered and failed dismally in an unbroken string of military ventures in recent decades, from the Bay of Pigs to "Desert One." The helicopter escapade finished whatever was left of America's military reputation. The French newspaper *Le Monde* asked, "What should we think of a military apparatus upon which the security of half the world depends and which can't fly two airplanes from a stretch of desert before the enemy has even been engaged?" Who can be deterred by a country that has bowed to deliberate provocations, accepted humiliations for years and remained idle when its declarations that an opponent's actions were "intolerable" were blandly ignored?

A report from Tokyo suggested: "It is American willpower, not power itself, that generates the most serious doubts. To many analysts, the decisive change is not numbers of warships or airplanes but uncertainty about American response—by the government or broad public opinion—in a military showdown."

In his latest book *The Real War*, Richard Nixon wrote:

> In the 1980s America for the first time in modern history will confront two cold realities. The first of these is that if war were to come, we might lose. The second is that we might be defeated

without war. The second prospect is more likely than the first, and almost as grim.

The Real War will probably not draw the attention it deserves because its author was thoroughly discredited by his actions in the Watergate affair. But his warnings should be taken with the utmost seriousness.

The Soviets probably are not planning to start a war with the United States. Feeling certain that time is on their side, they hope that a war may in the end not be necessary. They believe that they will achieve their immutable aim of world domination without a war if the trends of the past two decades continue long enough. "The Soviets have a momentum in every area from strategic nuclear, to projection forces, to naval forces . . ." Air Force Chief of Staff General Lew Allen told a congressional panel recently. They have been taking the initiative in several crucial areas in Africa and Asia and not been exactly idle in Europe nor Central and South America. They were able to do so with impunity, save for verbal expressions of our displeasure, which they ignored. The United States may some day soon be in no position to oppose, prevent, resist or undo action jeopardizing or severely damaging our vital interests or security which our adversaries may choose to take anywhere in the world. We may be unable to reject any demands they may raise in an ultimatum.

American military might reached its apex in World War II and has been on the downgrade ever since, falling dangerously behind in many crucial areas. The United States dismantled its defense establishment between 1945 and 1948, quickly cutting outlays from $81 billion to $13 billion. That unilateral disarmament prompted aggressive action in Korea in which we barely escaped military disaster. The defense budget then quickly quadrupled but resumed its downward trend in 1954, only briefly interrupted in the second half of the 1960s by the Vietnam action.

Widespread opposition to a strong defense establishment grew in the euphoric days of Camelot, New Frontier and Great Society, and became dominant during the Vietnam war. In no way could the enormous expansion of domestic programs have been financed except by diminishing the share of defense. Most Americans never understood what our military intervention in Southeast Asia was all about until *after* the Viet Cong took over South Vietnam and expanded its aggression to Laos and Cambodia, by which time it was far too late for effective counteraction. The Vietnam war was fought with the

American forces' right arm tied behind their back. A strategy which refrained from pursuing the most obvious course to victory—to shut off supplies to the aggressors by air, land and sea—was self-defeating, a futile and inexcusable drain on American lives and material resources. It wore out the public's patience with a war that could not be won by the means employed and generated a broad aversion to the military as such which divided the nation and sapped its strength. As our other ill-planned ventures, the Vietnam action ended in a debacle because of a lack of will, not a lack of power.

But the lack of will was soon translated into diminished power. The defense share of the federal budget dropped from two-thirds to one-fourth over the past quarter century, from 13.5% of GNP to 5.0% while the Soviet Union boosted military allocations to 13%—and, according to William T. Lee—to 18% of its GNP. The federal government spent in the early 1950s about four times as much on the military as on domestic services. By the late 1970s it allocated nearly three times as much to domestic benefits as to national defense. That left us with "Swiss cheese" defenses.

Representative Les Aspin (Colo.), author of several amendments to reduce military appropriations, in 1973 appealed to other members of Congress to go to work on their colleagues and "convince them that you've got to cut the defense budget if you want sufficient money for your own programs." The implication of this approach—that domestic outlays are a congressman's "own" programs while national defense is someone else's concern—well expressed sentiment at the time.

Congress acted in keeping with the general attitude of the public. After regularly boosting presidential recommendations on national defense appropriations in the early 1960s, it began cutting them in 1968 and reduced the military budget requests of the Nixon and Ford administrations by about $50 billion between 1969 and 1976. Jimmy Carter campaigned in 1976 on a promise to cut the defense budget and after becoming president redeemed his promise. With the aid of a like-minded Congress about $40 billion were taken from President Ford's defense plans between 1976 and 1980. This was carried out mainly by slowdowns (stretch-outs) on the MX missile, Trident submarine, carrier and other naval building programs and veto of the manned bomber and neutron bomb.

By the later 1970s the federal government was allocating a smaller share of its resources to national defense than ever before, except in the 1870s to 1890s, and a smaller percentage of GNP than at any time since prior to World War II. Our armed forces sank to less than half those of the USSR, and to the lowest numbers in three decades, as did defense production by American industry.

Gradually, in the course of the 1970s, it began to dawn on the American people and their representatives in Congress that they had placed the United States in the greatest peril it had ever been in. While American armed forces were growing weaker and their equipment increasingly inadequate, the Russians had been rearming at a rapid pace for nearly twenty years and their military machine was outspending and outbuilding us every year "to buy guns, planes, tanks, ships, and nuclear missiles."

The Soviet leaders' attitude decisively changed from what it was in the days of the Cuban missile crisis in 1962. Their responses to American protests against some of their actions gave clear testimony to awareness of their newly won strength and manifest American deficiencies. So did the behavior of the governments of many other countries which realistically reevaluated the shift in the balance of global power.

The American people also sensed that we were embarked on a course leading straight to disaster. The percentage of respondents to Gallup Polls who thought that we were spending too much on defense fell from 52% in 1969 to 14% in 1980 and half the replies expressed a belief that the military was not getting enough.

How much is "enough"? President Carter, whether because he saw the light or because he felt the heat, reversed course in 1978 and established a goal of 3% annual increases in defense appropriations (in *constant* dollars) which, in response to NATO pressures, he later upped to 5% but never fully implemented. His budget for FY 1981 showed very small boosts, raising national defense from 5.1% of GNP in 1978 and 1979 to 5.3% by 1983.

More money alone will not give our defense establishment all it needs. But without a great deal more money, we will certainly not be able to reach even a minimum required level of safety.

A 5% annual increase in funds will not even begin to "catch up" with the enormous lag that has developed over the past decade or two. A goal of 8% to 10% of GNP for defense for an indefinite number of years may be the minimum, if our military is to be placed in a position of being able to provide reasonable protection for the American people. Eight to ten percent of GNP equals the share of our resources allocated to defense in the 1950s and 60s—between the Korean and

Vietnam wars. Budget deficits then averaged less than $3 billion a year and inflation ran below 2%.

But the situation is now different. Domestic spending has grown by the equivalent of nearly 10% of GNP, with most of the funds derived from a commensurate cut in the share of defense and the rest from creating a budget deficit which now averages 2% of GNP. How could a boost in defense spending of 3% of GNP or more be financed? A major tax boost appears extremely unlikely at this time, as does a deliberate increase in the budgetary deficit. We should of course do everything in our power to spur economic growth and thereby augment governmental revenues at lower tax rates. But we cannot bank on being able to push economic expansion sufficiently to yield the enormous funds we need. That leaves only one alternative: a shift in funds from domestic benefits to defense equaling 3% of GNP or more, thereby reversing a fraction of the shift that took place between the 1950s and the 1970s.

That will not be easy. With more than four-fifths of federal domestic outlays now consisting of "entitlements" and other "uncontrollable" items, the political feasibility of such a drastic shift appears doubtful.

But a *de facto* decision will have to be made soon, explicitly or implicitly, whether the United States is to have at least an approximation of national security in the years ahead or whether the runaway welfare state will be permittted to continue until it is brought to a sudden and possibly violent end by forces beyond our control. The question now before the American people is: are we ready to "reorder national priorities" as we did, in the opposite direction, a quarter century ago? Has the sequence of dismal failures in recent years and the threat of worse, the disclosure of our impotence, instilled a sufficient sense of urgency among Americans and their national leaders?

We are on the threshold of a new generation of weaponry for the automated battlefield of the future, of instruments of attack and defense which have four elements in common: they are highly sophisticated, cover a virtually unlimited range of possibilities, take many years to develop, produce, deploy, and they are exorbitantly expensive. We do not know as much as we need to—and ought to—about the progress the Russians are making in developing and readying novel and more powerful tools of destruction, and surely less than they know about our doings. That may partially be inevitable for citizens of an open society in which myriads of statistical data and other information are easily available and movement and communications throughout the country unrestricted and largely unobserved. Moreover, Congress, in the pursuit of its Watergate safaris, wrecked much of our intelligence networks, the morale, drive and effectiveness of CIA, military intelligence, FBI workers, and destroyed beyond repair any confidence their foreign counterparts, our allies or potential agents, could have in us. Small wonder that so many major foreign events catch us by surprise, unprepared and without a ready counter-strategy.

Numerous comparisons have been advanced in recent years between the military strength of the United States and the Soviet Union. No purpose would be served by engaging in this book in that numbers game that has been played for so many years, listing side-by-side the estimates and appraisals of the two superpowers' weapons inventories. But some of our most important and costliest procurement needs should be mentioned.

Procurement now claims about one-fourth of the total defense budget with research and development taking another ten percent.

Our overall strategy has long been based on a "triad" of nuclear forces: land-based intercontinental ballistic missiles (ICBMs), submarine-launched ICBMs, manned bombers. To protect land-based ICBMs against being knocked out by a surprise first strike, plans for the MX system have been developed: 200 ICBMs would be shuttled among more than 4,000 silos over a wide area (in addition to dummies) so that the enemy would never know just where to hit; the surviving missiles would be ready for retaliation to destroy the attacker's home base. Costs have been estimated at between $34 and $60 billion and could run much higher. The search still continues for a more cost-effective alternative.

Our manned bomber fleet is based on B-52s most of which date back to the 1950s and are older than some of the pilots who fly them. The youngest B-52s were built nearly two decades ago and the planes, though retrofitted and modernized, are obsolete. They are not adequate to meet our needs into the 1990s by which time a "stealth" bomber—presumably invisible to Soviet radar—might be built. Work on a new manned bomber—B-1 and its derivatives—had been going on for a dozen years when President Carter scrapped the plans in 1977 as too costly. The question now is whether we can afford to wait another dozen years or more to replace the ancient B-52s.

The first of 27 Trident submarines fitted with 24 4000-mile ballistic missiles packing 8 warheads each was scheduled to join the fleet in 1979 but may not be ready until 1982. The 18,000-ton vessel costing well over $1 billion continues to be the subject of fierce controversies.

Our fleet has been allowed to fall from over 1,000 vessels a dozen years ago to less than 500 and is now far outnumbered by the Soviet navy in every category but aircraft carriers. Fewer than half of our 13 flattops are fit for sea duty. We now have four Nimitz class nuclear aircraft carriers with new additions estimated to cost $4 billion each, aside from escort vessels for each that might add another $5 billion. The carriers are to form the base for a new multipurpose fighter, the F/A 18 which should begin in the 1980s to replace older models at a currently planned cost of over $25 billion.

The navy has historically been called our first line of defense and it is today more important than ever. The United States depends on imports for 90% or more of its diamonds, manganese, alumina, cobalt, and platinum, for half or more of its crude oil, nickel, potash, mercury, zinc, gold, for vital shares of silver, iron ore, etc. How can the United States maintain its independence unless it can keep sea-lanes and access to sources of raw materials open, as well as transport connections with its allies anywhere in the world?

Events in the Indian Ocean and Persian Gulf areas in 1980 demonstrated that a 1–1/2-ocean navy cannot meet three-ocean requirements. A major shipbuilding program has become an urgent necessity.

Construction has barely begun on the first of the new Aegis guided-missile cruisers with many more needed, each costing at least $1 billion. Sea- and air-launched cruise missiles—successors to the German V-2 rockets which came close to destroying London in World War II—are expected to become available by 1982, with 4500 planned to be built by 1987 at a cost of $9 billion. The CX military cargo plane is essential to make a Rapid Deployment Force possible which could quickly transport troops and heavy equipment, including large tanks, to wherever they are needed around the globe—and land at small airfields. A fleet of 200 CXs would cost at least $12 billion.

The XM-1 battle tank, the first new U.S. tank design in decades, is scheduled to come off the line in 1981 and may gradually replace the old M60 tank. Many thousands of XM-1s will be needed to cope with the far larger and powerful Russian tank force.

The Defense Department's 1981 acquisitions program listed and described 149 research and development and procurement programs on weapons systems for a total cost of $57 billion. Even that huge sum may not be enough to meet the rapidly growing challenge from overseas.

The most serious shortcoming in our defense preparedness may well lie not in hardware but in manpower. A relatively small shortfall in numbers hides a decline in quality. Not that numbers were unimportant. Too many noncommissioned or petty officers' and technicians' positions remain unfilled—thereby incapacitating ships and entire units. Reenlistments, the cornerstone of an effective military force, have been rapidly declining in all services, in the Navy from 92% in 1973 to 62% in 1979, in the Marine Corps simultaneously from 82% to 52%, largely because pay has not kept pace with wages for technical and other skills in the private economy. That mid-career exodus is more than our armed services can sustain for long. Also, there are not enough airplane pilots, navigators, engineers and physicians who find an officer's career attractive compared with alternative opportunities. Rapid turnover and repetitive training costs constitute an enormous drain.

Most ominous is the precipitous fall in the mental caliber of enlisted personnel. The percentage of new accessions in the lowest two mental categories (III and IV) jumped from 66% of all Army recruits in 1972 to 80% in 1979. Training rigor inevitably had to yield. Disturbed over reports that 45% of new recruits were in the lowest mental category (IV), Congress in 1980 imposed a 25% limit on accessions in category IV for 1981 and 1982 and 20% from 1983 on. This caused the secretary of defense to express doubts that recruitment goals would be met. Jeffrey Record of the Institute for Foreign Policy Analysis in Washington recently commented: "The result is a U.S. Army recruited largely from the unemployed and economically disadvantaged, deprived of the energy and talent of middle-class America . . . an army, in short, of declining human quality and material readiness."

Military service has not ranked very high in the American public's scheme of values for a long time and sank to a new low during the Vietnam war and in its aftermath. Our young generation has come to believe that freedom is a gift of nature that can be had for the asking; it has not been taught that freedom must be fought for, won and forever defended, at a supreme effort and, if need be, at a supreme sacrifice. Youth has not been inspired to regard military service to the nation as an honor to be sought and cherished.

Having come to a stage where the profession upon which the country's security and its protection from ambitious enemies rest, is held in low esteem, we must wonder how secure the country's future is.

Can we depend on armed forces with a large number of soldiers who regard the army mainly as an employer of last resort because they cannot land and keep a job in the open market? Increased pay is an essential part of an effort to lift the effectiveness of the services to a higher level. But more money is not the whole answer to the qualitative shortcomings of our military. If the able and the best among us disdain service to their country, the country's outlook is dismal indeed.

Demands for larger defense appropriations are often countered with charges of huge waste in the military. Many of those charges undeniably are justified. Time and again the Pentagon has tried to close unnecessary military bases—such as Fort Dix, N.J. quite recently—but was prevented from doing so by influential members of Congress. This parallels the approval of a half dozen A-7 attack planes for the Air National Guard which the Pentagon opposed, only to be overridden by Congress. Inflated wage rates mandated by the Davis-Bacon Act are pushing up the bills for construction which could be completed at a far lower cost.

There are many other forms of waste aggregating billions of dollars which inevitably slip into outlays totaling over $150 billion, affecting three million persons directly and several more millions indirectly. We can no more *eliminate* all waste than we could stop killing 50,000 people a year on our highways in any way but by quitting to drive motor vehicles altogether. We can try to *reduce* the toll on the highways—and we do—and we can and do try to cut down on waste that occurs in all large-scale operations, public or private. That is a painstaking, continuing process which needs to be strengthened—but not a valid argument against appropriating the funds required for an adequate defense.

Admittedly there are duplications in weapons systems research, development and procurement. In dreaming up, designing, testing new means of "getting more bang for the buck," making our hardware

100

more powerful and penetrating, inventors cannot possibly know in advance which of the multitude of possible weapons systems will eventually prove to be the most cost-effective. Much less can they know what our adversaries may think up and throw against us, how serious a threat their new weapons will be, and how they can be counteracted and destroyed. In domestic fields we may experiment for years, on a small scale, until we find the method that seems to be the most productive. What we actually did in many social programs was implement on a national scale ideas which were never proved to produce the desired and promised results. But in social fields we can try, and if necessary, try again.

We may never get a second chance in modern warfare. If we do not have an adequate defense against a major new weapons system which an adversary may use against us, we may not get another opportunity. Many battles and wars in history were lost, and a nation's life span prematurely ended, when its opponent succeeded in overcoming it in an unexpected manner for which it was not prepared.

Duplication is expensive. But it may be essential in warfare and sometimes the lesser of two evils—the alternative being ultimate defeat.

Is there a possibility for a resurgence or "renaissance" of American military strength? There always is—until the final battle is lost. The Carter administration's plans in 1980 envisaged a trillion dollar defense outlay over the succeeding five years, the Senate Budget Committee projected $1.25 trillion while others suggested $1.5 trillion. A resurgence will cost a great deal of money. But we cannot simply *spend* ourselves out of the hole in which decades of neglect have left us.

What has been missing more conspicuously than enough hardware in recent developments involving Iran, Afghanistan and other trouble spots, is will to act decisively. Irving Kristol recently commented on American policies:

> By failing to enunciate (or even, apparently, perceive) the true nature of the problem, the Carter Administration has written one of the most humiliating pages in the history of American foreign policy. And by wasting a full year with lamentations and empty moralistic protestations, it has made it less likely that anyone in Iran—or elsewhere—now takes us seriously. This has been a disservice not only to the hostages but to all American personnel

101

stationed abroad, and is a disaster for our position as a world power. [*Wall Street Journal*, January 13, 1981.]

Our enemies believe and from past experience have reason to expect that, faced with crucial and perilous alternatives, America is likely to choose the path of quiet submission rather than of courage and risk. Iran's chief negotiator told its parliament on January 14, 1981: "We have rubbed the United States' nose in the dirt." Having been shown that this can be done with impunity, our adversaries anywhere may act accordingly and raise the level of their demands and provocations. Repeated and cowardly suffered humiliation has left a stain on America's honor. In our treatment of Iranian aggressive barbarism we focused our sights on the rescue of 53 hostages and danger to a possible expeditionary force rather than on the long-range security of 226 million Americans. We may have to pay a high price for it. If we cannot or dare not face the Iranians—can we or will we ever stand up to the Russians? John Kennedy did in 1962—but that seems ages ago, when the United States acted from strength and not from weakness.

Conclusion

The welfare state controversy is not waged over the question whether unfortunate and needy people ought to be kept from starving. It is not an argument on whether the state should aid families and individuals who demonstrably are unable to earn the necessities of life through gainful employment. That has long been settled in the affirmative and decisively so. The question is how far the state can go in transferring huge resources, which now exceed one-third of our total product, and redistribute enormous amounts of income, without inflicting serious damage on the nation: a weakening of incentives and efforts, slower economic growth, high-rate inflation, tight regulation of people's lives and interference with the normal conduct of business, intensifying social problems and internal conflicts that undermine and threaten to destroy peaceful life and the very fabric of our society. There is now overwhelming evidence that a well-intentioned but misguided welfare state has gone too far, that some of its programs, far from helping to alleviate our social problems, have aggravated them and made them well-nigh insoluble. Above all: the insatiable demands of the "wayward" welfare state have been crippling the strength of our national defense.

It is the ill-conceived experiments, the excesses and abuses of the welfare state in recent decades, not the idea of the welfare state as such, which have led to increasing demands that some of its counterproductive programs and activities be curbed or curtailed.

Six years ago, in the conclusion of this book's predecessor *The Growth of American Government* I ventured a prediction that,

> . . . the harvest of the wave of social legislation of the 1960s, of the new or enlarged programs, has been so disappointing that resistance to unlimited expansion of governmental activities and intervention is likely to become stronger as time goes on.
>
> The trend toward bigger government—in terms of heavier taxes, bigger spending, greater employment, tighter regulations of business and personal activities—therefore has a good chance of flattening out in the last quarter of the twentieth century.

It is now evident that the trend toward increased governmental spending for domestic purposes slowed substantially during the second half of the 1970s. This was due less to the intents of our political leaders than to lack of money. A main source of social program funds, the defense budget, hit rock bottom in the 1970s and could not be slashed further without catastrophic consequences; budgetary deficits reached levels which could not be pushed up more without driving inflation rates beyond the two-digit levels they had reached; given the prevailing public sentiment, taxes could be raised only by intricate methods which hid from the general taxpayer all or most of the boost, as was done in the case of the oil windfall profits tax and the 1977 social security tax increase.

The extraordinary growth of governmental spending of the 1960s slowed down in the past few years, but it was not halted, let alone reversed.

Social programs build their own clientele groups which organize for political effectiveness and fight to the utmost to keep the money flowing at an undiminished, and if possible increased, pace. Growth of the largest expenditure item, (income) transfer payments, is built into the federal budget by "entitlements" and statutory formulas which are hard to control and appear almost impossible to change, at least in a downward direction.

Enormous claims on the U.S. Treasury have been institutionalized and constitute a perpetual drain—which some would call a hemorrhage. Public opinion polls favor a reduction in the size of government but reveal little enthusiasm for drastic cuts in specific domestic services and benefits except possibly in public assistance. That makes a flattening of governmental growth tendencies likely to continue but keeps prospects of major reductions in doubt.

If we define attitudes toward the magnitude of government in terms of the political right and left—or as conservative and liberal, inappropriate though these labels may be etymologically—a shift to the right is evident. Gallup polls which revealed a 50:50 division among the Americans who labeled themselves conservative or liberal during the Vietnam-Watergate period, have reverted to an earlier 60:40 conservative majority.

Political events appear to confirm this. A shift to the right would have become obvious in the first half of the 1970s—fueled by disillusionment with the harvest of some of the Great Society ventures —if its manifestation had not been delayed by the Watergate scandal. Jimmy Carter, the most conservative among fourteen candidates in the 1976 democratic primaries, proclaimed opposition to big government in Washington a main theme of his campaign, and won. He beat a more conservative competitor, Mr. Ford, in the succeeding presidential election with a margin that was surprisingly narrow, considering the lingering effect on Republicans of the Watergate debacle as well as of the 1975–76 recession. President Carter won his party's nomination in 1980 with no liberal contender becoming a serious threat in the primaries or the presidential campaign though old-line liberals kept denouncing him as too conservative. Mr. Carter was beaten decisively in November 1980 by an opponent who clearly was much to his right. That was the direction in which public sentiment had been moving for some time and apparently wanted to go.

The staff of the *Washington Post* which can hardly be suspected of harboring a right-wing bias interpreted the meaning of the November 1980 election in the epilogue to a volume *The Pursuit of the Presidency 1980*: "In their own minds the mandate [the voters] gave to Reaganites was a mandate to control government spending, to control inflation, and to create a stronger military force. They were not demanding that the federal government be dismantled, that the United States should enter into foreign adventures, or even that taxes should be cut."

Constraint on total government spending and a stronger military mean a smaller share for domestic, mostly social, programs, which is the core of the platform of the political right, now apparently adopted also by the "mainstream."

One of the country's best-known socialist leaders, Michael Harrington, said on the Stanford campus in January 1981 that the November 1980 election was a "fundamental turning point" in that it marked the "end of Rooseveltian liberalism." That may overstate the case. Some of Roosevelt's programs such as old age insurance and unemployment insurance, stood the test of time, are no longer controversial—at least in principle—and will certainly be with us for a long while. Some of the later excesses and abuses which several of Franklin Roosevelt's successors inflicted on the country, with the help of cooperative Congresses, could be rectified in consequence of the 1980 elections.

As we are rapidly approaching the ominous year 1984, *Big Brother* indeed is watching us closely. But he could in 1984 and subsequent years loom far smaller than a straight projection of trends in the 1960s and early 1970s might have suggested. Steven R. Weisman illustrated in a penetrating *New York Times Magazine* (August 31, 1980) article "What is a Conservative?" how political attitudes have changed.

> Four years ago, the Democrats pledged to cut the military budget; this year they assail the Republicans for not having increased it more when they were in office. . . .
>
> A few decades ago a liberal was someone who opposed the use of racial, religious or ethnic quotas in jobs and education. Today someone who opposes quotas or affirmative action for blacks or Hispanics or other minorities in college, medical school or the work force is considered by many to be a conservative. . . .
>
> After many decades of spreading government, even many liberals find themselves turning today to the conservative solution of easing regulations and reducing the burden of taxes on business to spur productivity, investment and expansion.

Those changes in attitude began to develop as the economically and socially counterproductive consequences of a policy which primarily focused on redistributing income could no longer be hidden. The wayward welfare state redefined equity—an essential component of public policy—as meaning and requiring equality. In his Howard University speech of June 4, 1965, President Johnson identified the goal of his Great Society: "We seek . . . not just equality as a right and a theory but equality as a fact and a result." From promoting equal opportunity, government shifted to demanding equal results and created what David Lewis Schaefer called a *New Egalitarianism*, which led the welfare state astray and turned wide sections of the public against it. It replaced the pursuit of greater achievements through excellence with a drive for the lowest common denominator.

The point may best be illustrated by examples from the field of education. Studies by the National Institute of Education, which the nation's press widely reported, noted with great satisfaction that the "gap" between students from socioeconomically high-ranking and low-ranking backgrounds on standard tests of basic skills had materially narrowed. What the stories downplayed, if they mentioned it at all, was that the results did not so much reflect higher scores of the low-scoring groups but lower scores of the high-scoring groups. Greater equality was indeed achieved—but at what price!

In a brilliant article, Chester E. Finn, Jr., a longtime assistant to Senator Daniel Patrick Moynihan and an education expert, explained why he now calls himself "a semi-retired participant in the liberal consensus":

> . . . the liberal consensus today reveals a preoccupation with questions of educational equity and equality and a pronounced lack of interest in the issues of quality. . . .
>
> . . . the liberal consensus today has a generalized abhorrence of tests and other measures of educational achievement. . . .
>
> . . . the liberal consensus today is fixated on the concept of "need" and apathetic if not actually hostile to the concept of ability. . . .
> [*Change*, September 1980.]

Mr. Finn's charges against the "liberal consensus" are too extensive to be repeated here in detail. But the basic idea is clear and may help to explain why enormously expanded financial support of the public schools was followed by a consistently declining level of learning.

Theodore H. White once defined: "A liberal is a person who believes that water can be made to run uphill." If, for reasons of its own, water refuses to run uphill, a body of water located on a higher level must be made to run downhill, which is far easier to accomplish. The final goal of egalitarian policy is that all water—or people—must be on the same level, and if that level can't be high then it simply must be low. Unfortunately, by the laws of physics, water located at a lower level will generate less energy than water that is somewhere higher up.

106

The failure of our huge investment in education in recent decades to raise quality of performance, was repeated in numerous other social programs. That is why many of the early enthusiasts, who in the 1960s talked in the most glowing terms of the Great Society and its expected abundant dividends, have learned to refer to the programs' results in more guarded and qualified terms. Some of them, a declining number, still profess affection for egalitarian goals and policies and express hope that some day, somehow—if hundreds of additional billions of dollars were supplied—favorable results may be obtained.

Some of the transfer programs, to be sure, have been and continue to be eminently effective in redistributing enormous amounts of income from producers to nonproducers. This has sharply diminished the number of families and persons who by any reasonable standard can be labeled poor. Those programs have abolished poverty as a mass phenomenon in the United States and restricted its incidence to pockets of "insular" poverty, caused by individual circumstances or personal unwillingness to submit to the rules and demands of a twentieth century industrial society. We have not abolished, nor will ever be able to eliminate, the lowest ten percent or twenty percent on the income distribution scale. Thus the poor will truly always be with us—at least as long as we gauge poverty by a national average.

What the declining incidence of poverty has not brought about is a commensurate reduction in the incidence of social ills which, as claimed by egalitarians, were supposed to have been caused by poverty. Most of those ills—crime, tensions, violence, delinquency, family breakup and dozens of others—have multiplied, often at rates uncomfortably similar to the growth of the funds intended to combat them.

The egalitarian idea which spawned the wayward welfare state and its manifestations in hundreds of programs or features of programs, has an undeniable emotional appeal but unfortunately lacks a sense of reality. It is enormously expensive, not only in budgetary and tax terms but in the damage it has wrought, in the hopes it raised which were bound to be disappointed, in the dissensions and conflicts it created or intensified, in terms of an appalling weakening of the nation's economic and military strength and of its cohesion.

We cannot attain a necessary rate of economic growth without letting the carrot and the stick of the market work their way. We must allow adequate rewards for productive efforts, and not tax them away to satisfy envy among the less successful. We cannot protect from the stick those who will not respond to the carrot, without diminishing their motivation and sentencing them to perpetual dependency.

Sooner or later we shall have to recognize that we can have either liberty or equality, but we cannot have both. Equality was not, as some pretend, ordained by the Declaration of Independence which declared the Founders' belief that "all men are created equal." It did not say that all men will be or remain equal in economic or social status, regardless of individual and widely differing capacities, efforts and achievements.

Part of the cost of the wayward welfare state is manifested in a runaway, seemingly uncontrollable budget and in turn, in a rate of inflation that may ruin our economy and eventually our society.

A return to more sensible policies calls for a large number of changes, some of which are listed in the relevant chapters of this book. Leading among them is a reversal of the trend of shifting from guns to butter, a move that has made us too fat—and too weak to meet the challenges which face us now and will confront us in the future. Can necessary measures be adopted despite the strong opposition that can be expected from some of the beneficiaries of the current programs?

It will be difficult but not impossible. Congress may not be able to enact the necessary cutbacks unless adequate restraints are placed on its spending power by constitutional amendment. Congress may be unable to resist the multiplicity of special interest groups, each of which insists on its benefits and threatens each legislator with dire consequences unless it is given its pound of flesh. Congressman David Obey, chairman of the House Democratic Study Group was quoted by *Time* (February 23, 1981) as saying: "We are being eaten alive by the single-issue groups."

Congress' backbone could be strengthened by an amendment limiting federal spending—in *toto* or for nondefense purposes—to a set percentage of GNP or by requiring a balanced budget.

Experience of recent years makes it appear doubtful that Congress will pass such an amendment. It may have to be proposed by a constitutional convention—called by resolution of at least 34 state legislatures—and adopted by consent of 38 legislatures. About thirty legislatures have adopted resolutions calling for a constitutional convention, but they are not identical and their constitutional validity has been questioned.

Some believe that return to a gold standard could prevent reckless spending and would restore an economic balance, besides a sound currency. It conceivably might, but a Congress which lacks the discipline to keep its appropriations within revenues, is extremely unlikely to tie its hands by going to a gold standard. Nor could a drive for a gold standard attract as much support among the state legislatures and the people as demand for a balanced budget or a spending restriction which, as mentioned before, so far has been unable to amass the necessary popular strength.

There are, to be sure, other means of restraining the spending power of Congress. Most states require a popular vote for the incurrence of public debt, many state constitutions include provisions permitting *direct* legislation by their citizens through popular initiative, referendum or vetoes of tax boosts. It seems that we have put the muzzle on the wrong dog. Citizens have more power to control their state and local governments than the national government which, in important respects, has been beyond popular control for some time. If *government by the people* is to become a reality, a national referendum should be required for the incurrence of debt and tax boosts (except in specified cases of national emergency) and be allowed for other purposes through national initiative—if demanded by a qualifying minimum number of citizens. That could place the muzzle on the dog which, judging from long experience, needs to be restrained from putting too heavy a bite on us.

Limitations on federal spending through a constitutional amendment or the authorization of popular initiative and referendum at the federal level are of course merely techniques to achieve an end. They are not ends in themselves. The crucial question is not whether an amendment to balance the budget can be slipped into the U.S. Constitution by intricate methods, but whether the American people are satisfied with current trends or whether they want to stop the country's slippage and gradual deterioration of recent decades. If they are ready to settle for what they have been getting ever since the end of World War II, nothing will be able to stop the gradual decline and eventual demise of the American Commonwealth, probably before its third centennial. That may be a final and negative answer to Abraham Lincoln's question "whether this nation or any nation so conceived can long endure."

If, however, the American people wish to restore the nation's unbounded strength, confidence and security, the unquestioned

109

supremacy and global leadership role it held and enjoyed but a short while ago, they will find a way to accomplish it by electing to office the type of men and women with that goal foremost in mind and with the capacity to carry those ideas to a triumph; and the people will be willing to make whatever sacrifices that goal may require.

* * * * * * * * * * * * * * * * * * Notes

1. Roger A. Freeman, "The Wayward Welfare State," *Congressional Record*, October 5, 1970; *Vital Speeches of the Day*, October 15, 1970; *Modern Age*, Fall 1971.

2. Solomon Fabricant, *The Trend of Government Activity in the United States Since 1900* (New York: National Bureau of Economic Research, 1952).

3. M. Slade Kendrick, *A Century and a Half of Federal Expenditures* (New York: National Bureau of Economic Research, 1955).

4. Somerset Maugham, *Strictly Personal* (Garden City, N.Y.: Doubleday, Doran & Co., 1941), p. 216.

5. David A. Stockman, "The Social Pork Barrel," *Public Interest*, Spring 1975.

6. In constant dollars $12 billion were worth less in 1952 than $7 billion were in 1939.

7. John Kenneth Galbraith, *The Affluent Society* (Boston: Houghton Mifflin, 1958).

8. George Katona, *The Mass Consumption Society* (New York: McGraw-Hill, 1964), p. 62.

9. *Public Papers of the Presidents of the United States*, Lyndon B. Johnson, Book I, 1963–64 (Washington, D.C.: U.S. Government Printing Office, 1965), p. 822.

10. Henry J. Aaron, *Politics and the Professors* (Washington, D.C.: Brookings Institution, 1978), p. 1.

11. *Public Opinion*, October/November 1980, p. 2

12. *Social Security Bulletin*, November 1980, p. 32.

13. For a list see: *An Inventory of Federal Income Transfer Programs, Fiscal Year 1977* (White Plains, N.Y.: Institute for Socioeconomic Studies, 1978), eds. William J. Lawrence and Stephen Leeds.

14. Daniel P. Moynihan, "The Crisis in Welfare," *Public Interest*, Winter 1968.

15. Donald Lambro, *Fat City, How Washington Wastes Your Taxes* (South Bend, Ind.: Regnery/Gateway, 1980), pp. xvii, 2.

16. Murray L. Weidenbaum, *Costs of Regulation and Benefits of Reform* (St. Louis: Washington University, 1980); and idem., *The Future of Business Regulation* (New York: Amacom, 1979).

17. Peter F. Drucker, "The Danger of Excessive Labor Income," *Wall Street Journal*, January 6, 1981.